MEDITATION
and
MY THOUGHTS
on
LIFE

MEDITATION
and
MY THOUGHTS
on
LIFE

Audrey W. Mills

XULON PRESS

Xulon Press
2301 Lucien Way #415
Maitland, FL 32751
407.339.4217
www.xulonpress.com

Table of Contents

Acknowledgments

- To my husband, Reverend Wilbert Mills, Sr., I thank God for giving us an abundant life together in our approaching sunset years. God has put the pieces of our lives together.
- God has truly blessed me with a great family life, new and old, and a great church family and fellowship at The People's Community Baptist Church (TPCBC), Silver Spring, Maryland under the pastoral ministry of Reverend Dr. Haywood Robinson, III. Because of you, my thoughts stay focused on how good God is and His amazing grace.
- Thanks to all persons in the chapter "Stalwart Men and Women of God" for providing information about your lives for me to describe them by using an acrostic (the use of an acrostic for this book is to compose writing from the initial letters of your name).
- Thanks to my daughter, Andrea Hines, my son-in-law, Stevie Hines, and my granddaughter, Shayla Hines, for being consultants, which relieved me from many worries.

- I thank God most of all, because, without God, I wouldn't be able to do any of this.
- The Holy Spirit, my teacher, also gave me ideas every day.
- A special thank you to Shirley France for suggesting that I write my next book on *Meditation and My Thoughts on Life*. Your insight and wisdom led me to thoughts on life, faith, and trust.
- A special thank you to Matthew Coates, owner of Photography by Madison in Laurel, Maryland, for photography editing services to meet photo publishing requirements.
- A special thank you to the following people for being great encouragers for me to keep on writing.
  - Cynthia Marshall-McFarland and Damon McFarland
  - Daniel and Keely Wilson
  - Derek and Sheilita Jones
  - Helen Hines
  - Lloyd and Josie Porter
  - Orlando and Adrienne Smith
  - Mary and Joseph Summersville, you are stars in my crown. You always have encouraging words for me to move forward when God gives me an assignment to complete.
  - A special thank you to my cousin, Marilyn Walton, who is a loyal supporter and encourages me to keep writing.

Introduction

I wrote this book because I want to tell the world that God's way of life is better than ours. The Bible says that God's way is perfect, refreshing, trustworthy, right, and enlightening (Ps. 19:7-8).

When you feel like your life is a mess, God works all things for your good (Rom. 8:28). When you feel like your life is going great, God has greater things in store for you (1 Cor. 2:9). When you feel like your life is falling apart, God is your strength and deliverer (Ps. 18:1-2). When you feel like your life is over the top amazing, there is a place to direct your gratitude (James 5:13). God's way for your life is the best possible way you can live. It's the life God intends for us to live.

Everything good or bad that comes into our life is because of who we are. We must create a world where life is an ever-increasing journey of happiness. When we are sure that we are on the right road, there is no need to plan our journey too far ahead. No need to burden ourselves with doubts and fears as to the obstacles that may bar our progress. We cannot take more than one step at a time. Most of the unhappiness in the world ends if we can control our minds. Getting our spiritual life in the right direction is of utmost importance if we are to have peace of mind and happiness throughout our life.

Each chapter of the book gives you suggestions on how you can reach your goals. Scripture passages are an integral part of each chapter.

The True Story of Life

Have you ever stopped to think about why God created the world? Have you ever stopped to think about what God's story is about life? When we read God's Word in the Bible, it tells us that Jesus is the true story of the whole world. When God created the world we came into existence by the Father, the Son, and the Spirit. Humanity was designed by God to experience a relationship of trust with God. The first humans were enticed by the powers of evil. They used their freedom to choose their path and to be their own gods. This decision created brokenness with God, the Creator. Despite this brokenness, God did not destroy the world. God did the unthinkable: He took on human form in Jesus, a Jewish man from Nazareth. Jesus's entry into the world embodied the fullness of God and modeled for Israel and the rest of the world what it looked like to be in the right relationship with God. Jesus taught and preached to the people to turn away from being their own god and urged them to turn to the one true God. He taught about living in love, service, and humility rather than with dominating power and selfishness. He taught about another world that would replace the world of humanity. Jesus's message upset the powers of both the Jewish leaders of Israel and the Roman Empire. As a result, He was executed as a criminal for insurrection by way of crucifixion, suffocating to death while hanging from a wooden cross. What seemed to be a failed cause became the greatest victory to mankind. Three days later, God raised Jesus from the dead. His resurrection was the real deal.

His followers came to believe that in the death of Jesus, God provided a way for the world to be healed. Through Jesus's death, God took all of humanity's brokenness upon himself, through Jesus on the cross.

At the cross, God defeated the powers of evil that enticed humanity. Those who trusted Jesus's work on their behalf could experience the right relationship with God as a gift from God to undeserving people.

After Jesus rose from the dead, He returned to the loving community of God, promising to come back and make the world right for good. Jesus had commissioned His followers to share the purpose of His death and resurrection with the rest of the world.

The restoration of the world will take place upon Jesus's return.

He promised to restore the world. Brokenness will be eradicated. The powers of evil will be stamped out for good. Pain and suffering will end. This world will be transformed into a new world where we'll enjoy the loving relationship with God and each other. We must have the faith to believe that this is true. The restoration of the world is recorded in the scriptures. We should have the faith to believe that God's story is true about life.

Life is a Journey of Ups and Downs

*L*ife is a journey with mountains, valleys, and everything in between. It is our perspective toward circumstances and situations that impact the course of our lives.

We must accept the fact that life is not permanent, but temporary and we have to live one day at a time.

Live your life each day, as you would climb a mountain. Climb slowly, steadily, enjoying each passing moment. Enjoy the view, but most of all, thank God for another step in life and for the gift of life.

As we journey through life, fly high like an eagle. Spread your wings and soar high. Be an eagle Christian. Isaiah 40:31 tells us, "But they that wait upon the Lord shall renew their strength; they shall mount up with wings as eagles; they shall run, and not be weary; and they shall walk, and not faint."

God has a way of getting us to leave our comfort zone. He doesn't want us to depend on other believers all our lives. He causes us to leave our comfort zone and learn to fly to high places. To live in high places, we must learn to wait on God.

When we go through the storms of life, be like the eagle, circle higher toward the sky. Like the eagle, if you encounter a storm, set your wings and fly directly toward the storm. The velocity of the wind will lift you safely above the storm. This is what the Scriptures mean when it says that believers mount up with wings as eagles.

Life is a series of experiences with major goals such as happiness, success, meaning, and integrity.

When we serve other people to improve their lives, this is a goal many psychologists label and refer to as happiness, a pleasant life, and a meaningful life.

Luke 12:15 (NLT) states, "Beware! Guard against every kind of greed. Life is not measured by how much you own."

As Christians, we should build a life that pleases God. Colossians 1:10-12 (NLT) says, "Then the way you live will always honor and please the Lord, and your lives will produce every kind of good fruit. All the while, you will grow as you learn to know God better and better." The power source of life is when you focus on the Word.

The Power of the Fruit of the Spirit In Our Life

*M*ost people want power, but they search for help in the wrong places. Some believe they have an inner psychic power they can uncover and unleash. Many people put their hopes in one of the false religions, either non-Christian or counterfeit Christian. What mankind needs most is spiritual power from our Creator God. The force He offers can govern our lives, solve our problems and lead us to real peace. This spiritual power is the Holy Spirit from our Creator God. The Holy Spirit is not something we are born with. It can only be received as a divine gift from God after one believes the truth of the Bible, repents of one's sins, and is baptized for the forgiveness of sins (Acts 2:38-44).

The Bible shows that the Holy Spirit is the nature and essence of God the Father and His Son, Jesus Christ. In fact,

"God is Spirit" (John 4:24 GNT) and the source of the Holy Spirit. John 4:24 states, "God is a Spirit; and they that worship him must worship him in spirit and in truth."

God's Spirit profoundly changes people. Paul wrote, "...the fruit of the Spirit is love, joy, peace, longsuffering, gentleness, goodness, faith, Meekness, temperance..." (Gal. 5:22-23).

As Christians, we can live out the fruit of the Spirit in our life.

Faith...

Believe the promises of God in the face of extreme difficulties. When things don't go right, go to the Bible and read, "...all things work together for good to them that love God, to them who are called according to his purpose" (Rom. 8:28). Then don't just believe it, but tell yourself, "How differently would I react if I knew beyond a shadow of a doubt that this was true?" Watch your faith take shape in your words and your behavior.

Goodness...

We can be so quick to assume the worst, but remember; good things can and do happen at any time. Be on the lookout for miracles. Share stories about answered prayers. When you look out for the good things in life, you'll see Psalms 23:6 come alive as goodness follows you everywhere you go.

Peace...

There is a river of peace that flows inside of you when you are still long enough to feel it. Every day, carve out five minutes of silence. Perhaps, it's first thing in the morning. Put the phone away or anything that is a distraction. Sit somewhere without any distractions and focus on your breathing. It may take time for your mind to stop racing, but once it does, you will be at peace throughout your entire body.

Meekness...

This fruit often gets mixed up with weakness, but in actuality, meek people are very humble. Try a dose of humility the next time you're in an argument. When you feel the urge to point out someone else's flaws, take a break. Try looking at the situation from the other person's point of view. Stop insisting and start listening. You'll find a cure for strife when you put on a spirit of meekness.

Gentleness...

Harsh criticisms and judgments can hurt. Proverbs 15:1 (NIV) reads, "A gentle answer turns away wrath, but a harsh word stirs up anger." If Christians are called to heal, then it begins with speaking to and treating others gently. The next time you have to give bad news or confront a friend about a problem, as Ephesians 4:15 says, "But speaking the truth in love, may grow up into him in all things, which is the head, even Christ."

Love...

Don't settle for a *Facebook* version of friendship. True love needs a personal touch. Show people in an unexpected way that you love them. Get a package of blank greeting cards and make a list of friends and family, especially the ones you don't see often. Write them a short note that shares how much you appreciate them.

Joy...

Joy comes from being with God. Joy is the smile we have inside, no matter what is happening around us. God is our source of joy. The more time we spend with God, the more we will have.

Long suffering...

Living in the Spirit and keeping all our evil tendencies on the cross, will enable us to gain this virtue little by little. People are conceited and stubborn, and it takes much leniency and patience to lead them to the goal.

Temperance...

Temperance means that you are in control and denotes power over one's self. It is often translated as the word *self-control*. It suggests the control or restraint of one's passions, appetites, and desires. Because the Holy Spirit has produced temperance in your life, you can say no to overindulging in fleshly activities.

Let us live out the fruit of the Spirit.

One's Thought Life

*O*ne's thought life is important because the happiness of your life depends on the quality of your thoughts. We can equate thinking with another form of nutrition. If we do not feed our thoughts, we wouldn't be able to maintain life. What we focus on the most in life grows. Many of us have experienced many ups and downs, and have gained an appreciation, sensitivity, and an understanding of life that fills us with compassion, understanding, and a deep loving wisdom.

The wisest, most loving, and well-rounded people you have ever met are likely those who have known misery, known defeat, known the heartbreak of losing something or someone they loved, and have found their way out of the depths of their despair. These people have experienced many ups and downs, and have gained an appreciation, sensitivity, and an understanding of life that fills them with compassion, understanding, and a deep loving wisdom. People like this aren't born; they develop slowly over time. Their struggles have strengthened them and given them an upper hand in this world.

When hard times hit, and the challenges you face are great, you can either let your situation define you, let it destroy you, or let it strengthen you. The choice is yours to make.

Let's remember that pain is part of life and love, and it helps you grow stronger even through the hardest times. Don't expect life to be wonderful all the time. In other words, life isn't perfect, but it sure is good. Our goal shouldn't be to create a perfect life, but to live an imperfect life in radical amazement. To get up every morning is a blessing. Every day is a gift. Never treat life casually. It's God's amazing grace. If you change your thoughts, you can change your mind set. Don't let fear stop you. Fear is only as deep as your mind allows. You are still in control. Don't let fear stop you from moving forward with your life. Remember, when you stop expecting things to be a certain way, you can appreciate them for what they are. You will realize that life's greatest gifts are rarely wrapped the way you expected.

Pray to God to help you turn your wounds and worries into wisdom. Remember, the price of happiness is responsibility. You are responsible for your happiness. Take control of your circumstances. Life is not lived where everything is perfect. It is lived here and now, with the reality of the way things are. Don't let the past and future steal your present. Appreciate your life. Thank God for waking you up each day. At the end of the day, it's not happiness that makes us thankful, but thankfulness that makes us happy.

Remember, you are valuable. You don't have to be flashy to be impressive. You don't have to be famous to be significant. You don't have to be a celebrity to be successful. You don't need to be validated by anyone else. You are already valuable. You just need to believe in yourself and what you wish to achieve.

Success is how you define it, not what everyone else says it must be for you.

Amid hard times, you are not alone. You are never alone when you pray to God to walk beside you. God is the answer.

Romans 12:2 (NKJV) tells us, "And do not be conformed to this world, but be transformed by the renewing of your mind..." This scripture reminds us that in life, we face challenges and difficulties. When we forecast that we can't do a certain thing even before the problem is encountered, you are defeating yourself and Satan is welcoming you to his army. An action plan is to *renew your mind* with God's Word. The power source of life is the Word of God. Life can be changed when you speak God's Word. God's Word is powerful. You can achieve true and lasting success through the Word of God. The image that God's Word will build inside you becomes the most powerful force in your life.

How do I know? In 2010, I was on a faith journey after a major operation was performed to remove a benign tumor cushioned on my spine in the neck area. Because of my positive thoughts and faith in God, my inner thought life transformed my life.

The Process of Biblical Meditation

*B*iblical meditation is a prayerful reflection where you ask the Holy Spirit to illumine your understanding as Jesus did with the disciples on the Emmaus Road (Luke 24:32). Meditation includes picturing, speaking, feeling, and study.

Meditation is the Holy Spirit using all faculties in man's heart and mind. Following is a seven-step meditation process from Communion With God Ministries.[1]

1. Write this verse in a meditation journal and keep it with you to meditate on throughout the day. "And it shall be, when he sitteth upon the throne of his kingdom, that he shall write him a copy of this law in a book out of *that which is* before the priests the Levites" (Deut. 17:18 AKJV). It is of great use for each of us to write down

what we observe as most affecting and edifying to us, out of the scriptures and good books, and out of the sermons we hear.

2. Quiet down. Become still in God's presence, loving Him through soft music and praying.

3. Reason together with God. "Come now, and let us reason together, saith the Lord: though your sins be as scarlet, they shall be as white as snow; though they be red like crimson, they shall be as wool" (Isa. 1:18). This scripture tells us to let the Spirit guide your reasoning process. Ask, "Lord, what do you want to show me about the context of the verse?"

4. Ponder the Scripture, speaking it to yourself over and over again until you can repeat the Scripture.

5. Pray that the Scripture reveals God's heart toward you.

6. Ask God to speak to you through the Scripture. Record the dialogue in a journal.

7. Act. Accept God's revelation and rebuke anything that stands in the way of implementing it. Then speak it forth and act on it.

Trusting God totally with our lives, knowing He is good, and will do what is best for us *is* faith. This trusting faith allows us to magnify God in our lives for the entire world to see. God's sovereignty directs human drama when Meditation and Prayer dialogue. When they dialogue, they send a message to uplift one's spirit.

I believe you will hear Meditation say, "When I speak, I tell people to listen to God and think through with Him. I let them know that when they think God's thoughts, they will find His will and viewpoint in order to discover truth. It is a time of giving God a chance to speak."

Prayer responds, "I also let people know that prayer is communion with God. Through meditative prayers, one can encounter the ultimate experience of your relationship with God and union with the Lord. Contemplative prayer also is being aware of the loving presence of God."

Meditation responds by saying, "I let others know that one should meditate daily on the Scriptures by letting the Word of God dwell in their life. They get to know God better when they meditate. The soul will learn to meet God in a meditative way because I'm special in one's life."

Prayer speaks out by saying, "I hear you Meditation, but I am also special because I'm the stairs that one must climb each and every day in order to reach God. When you reach Him in prayer, and ask Him to lighten your burdens, He will reply, because God is never beyond our reach."

Meditation retorts, "You are right Prayer, so let us both agree that there is nothing more memorable and more powerful than an encounter with God through meditation and prayer."

Meditation acknowledges its role by saying, "I have to be experienced by a person seeking to know God consciously and consistently until it becomes a habit. The habit of meditation is essential to Christian living."

Prayer responds, "I believe you, Meditation, therefore, let us both agree that prayer is powerful because it is conversing with the living God. Prayer is active trust, *faith in action.* Matthew 6:6-9, Ephesians 3:14, Philippians 4:6, and Colossians 1:12 are all Scriptures that describe the stronghold of prayer."

Meditation responds to Prayer by saying, "Thank you Prayer. We both believe that our thought life helps people understand that we are a gaze of faith fixed on Jesus. The most important way to discipline the mind, and thus connect with truth is to spend regular time in prayer and meditation with God."

The Holy Spirit guides the above process, leading to more or less emphasis on any of the various steps, according to God's desires for the present moment and the personal needs we have. Throughout the process, we should remain dependent upon the Holy Spirit, our teacher.

My Testimony About Prayer: Alone With God – Conversing With God

*S*pend time with the Lord in prayer. Prayer is the miracle we often take for granted, for in prayer, created beings communicate with the creator. Prayer is conversing with the living God.

Matthew 6:6 tells us to find a prayer closet, "But thou, when thou prayest, enter into thy closet, and when thou hast shut thy door, pray to thy Father which is in secret; and thy Father which seeth in secret shall reward thee openly."

Open up your heart and talk to God through His Word (Ps. 94:12, John 7:17).

Learn to be quiet with your mind and heart open to God for a period of time. Let God bring thoughts to you as you wait upon Him. Be in an attitude of dependent awareness.

Prayer is a two-way conversation between God the Father and one of us, His children.

One of my best friends was on my mind early one morning. I waited until eight a.m. to call her. The phone rang, and rang, and rang, but no answer. I kept dialing her number during intervals of time, but no answer. Later during the day, when she arrived home, she called because she checked her caller ID. I told her how God put her in my spirit that particular day. She replied, "I was at the optometrist's office and he told me that I am going blind and I have to have an emergency surgery. He also said that my cataracts also need to be removed."

I prayed the following prayer with her directed by the Holy Spirit.

Dear Heavenly Father,

We come before the throne of grace right now because we need You every minute, every hour, every day. Father, we seek You today in the face of trials and suffering. Father, give my sister the faith that shows her the way to rejoice in any circumstance. Father, because of Your sovereignty, and Your goodness toward us, we have the faith to believe that You are able to use every situation for the good in our lives.

We call upon You now to send forth Your miracle-working power to heal her eyes that need healing. Father God, command every cell, tissue, and muscle, to come to complete strength and harmony.

Father God, it is through You that we live and move and have our being. We have the faith to believe that You can recreate her now and restore her health.

Our mustard seed faith lets us know that You can fill us with Your healing power.

1 Peter 5:6 tells us, "Humble yourselves therefore under the mighty hand of God, that he may exalt you in due time."

You are the lily of the valley and the bright morning star, and You can heal her right now because You have the last move.

Amen.

The following week after the prayer, she called me and said, "Sister Mills, I just got back from the doctor. Based upon his examination now, he could not find any evidence of blindness.

Sister Mills, I can see from a distance a block long. I am still scheduled to have my cataract removed. Praise God!"

My friend was excited, exhilarated, and joyful in the Lord. God let both of us know that He had answered her in the secret places of her heart.

I thank God for His guidance. God tells us how to pray so that He can answer the prayer.

Never get in the habit of saying what God cannot do. There's nothing too hard for God. He is a God of might and miracles.

In a sense, all answered prayer is a miracle because the supernatural is moving into the natural. Any time prayer is answered, in the classic sense, that is supernatural.

Remember, in the Bible when miracles were performed,

1. They gave glory to God.
2. They did not glorify men.
3. They validated the claims or the identity of God, and
4. They advanced God's work significantly.

Spiritual Lifelessness

*C*hristians at all levels of spiritual maturity experience periods of spiritual lifelessness or stagnation. Rhonda Jones, creator of "The Christian Meditator" website and author of *The Christian Meditation Journal* states, "I would characterize spiritual lifelessness as being ignorant to the ways and moves of the Spirit in your life as well as your being. People are generally spiritually lifeless because they:

1. Don't know that God's spirit lives in them.
2. Aren't seeking to connect with the spirit within them.
3. Are distracted by the material and physical things of the world.
4. Are too busy to be still and create space for God's spirit to speak to them."[2]

God wants us to spend time with Him every day in prayer evaluating and reformulating long and short-term goals of life with Him. As we achieve our specific goals by God's grace, this should encourage us to expect God to do greater things in and through us.

Ways to Handle Spiritual Lifelessness or Dryness

Allen Parr of Allen Parr Ministries helps us understand there are times in our lives when we have a disconnected feeling from God, like we've lost our passion for our pursuit of Him. This feeling can lead us to feel stuck in our faith, not knowing how to find our way back on track.[3] Hebrews 12:1-2 (AKJV) can help us identify that feeling and learn how to blockade distraction and sin.

Key Points:

- Lay aside your weight
- Lay aside habitual sin
- Focus on Jesus
- Admit where you are
  Psalms 42:5-6 (NLT) says, "Why am I discouraged? Why is my heart so sad? I will put my hope in God? I will praise Him again--my Savior and my God..."[4]
- Live a life of purpose

When we feel we have very little to live for outside of our immediate family we begin to question whether our life is really counting for much. Are we making a difference? Am I living out exactly what God has called me to do?[5]

- Practice spiritual discipline - prayer, quiet time, worship, and fasting
  Even Jesus, who is God, understood the importance of getting away by himself to pray.
  Luke 5:16 (NLT) tells us that Jesus withdrew to the wilderness for prayer.[6]

Beware of Satanic Attack

The devil, or Satan, is real and personal. He attacks us primarily through our minds, for example, deception, accusations, and temptations, but also physically. These attacks can trigger periods of spiritual lifelessness, especially if we fail to recognize Satan's involvement.

We must be on the alert for and resist the devil (Matt. 26:41, Eph. 6:11, James 4:7, 1 Pet. 5:8-9).

Keep the faith that there is hope of escape from the particular complications surrounding your spiritual lifelessness in your Christian life.

Consequently, don't be ashamed of spiritual lifelessness and do not try to hide it from others behind an ever-ready, victorious life, Christian smile. That only grieves the Holy Spirit (the Spirit of truth - John 14:17) and raises additional barriers to honesty with others. Instead, talk about your lifelessness with a mature, understanding Christian friend.

Don't regard spiritual lifelessness as merely a sickness but a symptom of recovery. God's seeming far away can cause us to suffer only if at other times we have experienced His nearness. Suffering due to spiritual lifelessness is thus a sign that the Holy Spirit is present in us and contains the promise of new spiritual health.

God cares for us. We thank God for helping us from sinners to winners, for the wrong things that we do.

When we cry out, God sees us through darkness and hopeless times of life because of His love, we suffice.

Our daily walk with God and His Son, Christ, takes us to our next step of faith and grace.

The Holy Spirit, our teacher, teaches us His ways through His Word to help us face the hardships of life with vigor, strength, and inner peace with grace.

Divine Intervention

On August 16, 2015, the Holy Spirit awakened me in the wee hours of the morning. The Holy Spirit told me that my husband, Wilbert, and I had to have fellowship, socialization, and family unity with our daughter, son-in-law, and granddaughter. Before the intervention, I always worried about them traveling from Silver Spring, Maryland to Virginia Beach, Virginia on the busy, speedy Interstate 95/495 highway.

My husband and I discussed the Holy Spirit's directions. I told Wilbert we could get our own place but be nearby.

I called my granddaughter, Shayla, and told her that we would be up on October 22, 2015. She said, "Oh! Mom and Dad have been looking at houses." Hebrews 11:1 says, "Now faith is the substance of things hoped for, the evidence of things not seen." We sold our house and made permanent preparation to be together in Maryland.

Proverbs 16:9 states, "A man's heart deviseth his way: but the Lord directeth his steps."

The divine intervention in my life has greatly impacted my life and faith.

It is a wonderful thing when God takes over and it is not a checkmate. The King of kings always has another move and it is a winning move.

When God makes a move, love wins, hope wins, light overcomes darkness, courage overcomes fear, faith overcomes despair, and you are born anew to a living hope. It is Christ's finished work.

Christ's finished work will help us see the goodness of the Lord because He has already made available goodness to us (Rom. 1:8).

We will build our faith on God's reputation because He is our provider and He will provide. God can create anything. We don't need anything but God because God can make it rain without a cloud. He brought water out of a rock. God made Mary deliver Jesus as a virgin. Since God is good, we just believe. We don't have to figure it out because God knows how to bring good to life.

We will not violate or ignore God's will. The glory of God is ready for us to move the doubt out of the way. We will stand on the promises of God. The devil will always try to get you to doubt the promises of God. When Satan says defeat, we will say victory because God's truth defeats doubt every time.

The Fabrics of My Life

John Clayton, author of the *Does God Exist?* program website, desires to provide practical materials designed to answer questions. Mr. Clayton's thoughts helped me understand the fabrics of my life.

> "Fabric is tough stuff to produce, especially if the fabric is good, attractive, and durable... The fabric of life is very much the same. Life has to be planned..." like most fabrics.[7]

As a retired educator, I witnessed,

> "...children who had been born to mothers whose bodies were affected by alcohol, crack, and other substances. Planning to have a child cannot be overemphasized, and making sure

that life has a good physical start is of considerable importance."[8] A newborn "...baby is like a new piece of fabric...what the child hears, how they are treated, how and what they are taught affects...how their life will look as an adult... Trying to clean up a life which has been mutilated by sin and the problems of life is almost impossible without divine help."[9]

Consider the following passages highlighted by Mr. Clayton:[10]

- "Train up a child in the way he should go: and when he is old, he will not depart from it" (Prov. 22:6).
- "The rod of correction imparts wisdom..." (Prov. 29:15 HCSB).
- "Fathers, do not exasperate your children; instead, bring them up in the training and instruction of the Lord" (Eph. 6:4 NIV).
- "I have no greater joy than to hear that my children are walking in the truth" (3 John 1:4 NIV).

We are never alone in the world; therefore, we depend on others for more than just mere survival.

We comprise the real fabrics of our lives when we work with one another in creating unity in the family. Psalms 133:1 (NKJV) tells us, "Behold, how good and how pleasant it is for brethren to dwell together in unity!"

Father God, thank you for putting my family and people of all walks of life to make up the fabric of my life. My family and friends are my anchor.

They are the threads that hold me together.

To My Children
You Are The Fabrics of My Life

Andrea, my star of wonder.
Stevie, my adventurous world.
Shayla, my destiny child.
Wilbert Jr., deceased now, but was my anchor at all times.

Andrea, the fabric and thread that you have sown in my life has created hope, reality, and balance during my approaching sunset years.

Stevie, you sow good fabric in my life when I receive good advice from you. Your integrity and loyalty give me inner peace.

Shayla, your thread and fabric in my life are the happiness that you spread in me when you use the gifts that God has given you.

Wilbert Jr. (Bert), you are no longer with me, but your memory still lingers on. The thread and fabric you had sown in my life when I was a principal helped me with my career.

Your lives have greatly impacted my life with a vision to venture the unknown. Each of you travels across a galaxy of love landing inside my heart with the identity of a dove.

God points each of you to a horizon that promises great dividends for my life. Therefore, my children, with God's help, I will suffice.

Thank you for your star of wonder and your star of life, which has transmitted into my spirit and will last for a lifetime.

My Daughter, Andrea

Andrea Hines

A   Anchored in God's love each and every day.

N   Never complaining but moves to do it God's way.

D   Dreamers have dreams, and you are one of them, who move when God directs your path. What can I say?

R   Reach out, daughter, for directions from God's love and do not sway.

E   Enjoy the scenery that God provides.

A   Always remember when you walk with God, you are not alone, so keep on moving because God is always by your side.

My Stalwart Son-In-Law, Stevie

Stevie Hines

Stevie, you are a star of wonder and a star of might,
Who is blessed with God's wisdom, knowledge, and insight.

Under the shadow of God's wings, He has endowed you with strength and love that sings a song of change.

You are no longer called my son-in-law, but a son, raised up by God to carry a torch so others can see the bright light of love as a destiny.

Thank you, Stevie, for caring for me.

You are a stalwart son from A to Z.

My Granddaughter, Shayla

Shayla Hines

S   Starlight and star bright are shown in your beauty and in your life.

H   Hope and faith are available to you.

A   Always there to carry you through.

Y   Yield to God and move to higher grounds,

L   Longing always to take with you my legacy of love...
Love to go and conquer the world.
Love to learn all about the known and unknown things.
Love to be confident.
Love to be appreciative.
Love to be patient.
Love to love.
Love to like yourself.

A   Always remember to take with you a peg to hang your biggest hope.

My Deceased Son, Wilbert "Bert" Mills, Jr.

Wilbert Mills, Jr.

Our only son, Wilbert "Bert" Mills Jr., died September 23, 1999. However, since we have been apart, his memory lingers on as treasures in our hearts. His legacy of love, compassion, and strength are still being unfolded today, by those lives he touched as he passed their way.

On October 26, 2000, we received a Memorial Resolution in Bert's honor from the Commonwealth of Virginia for his contributions to the community. We are thankful to God for the life he lived. We miss him and cherish his memory.

My deceased son is still a fabric in my life.

To My Husband, Reverend Wilbert Mills, Sr.

Reverend Wilbert Mills, Sr.

You are the Fabric of My Life

W What a life God designed for you.

I It's in the Word of Prophet Isaiah, "This is the way, walk ye in it" (Isa. 30:21 NIV).

L Life is worth living when God plans your life. Why?

B Because you will suffice.

E Even when things look blight, God leads you to the Promised Land to give you insight about life.

R Regardless of the hardships, when things look dim and hopeless, new mercies from God will rescue you to follow through.

T This life you have lived was planned by God because of His love for you. I thank God for being the center of our life and for uniting us as husband and wife.

God, we give you all the glory. For without you, there would be no life story, of how you kept us together through thick and thin, darting satanic forces from without and within.

God, under your mighty hand, we are able to weather the wind and the storms when things go wrong. We endure life like the Lebanon tree that stands tall and strong.

We are approaching our sunset years and wanted to share our memories of your love and grace.

To God be the glory!

The Fabrics of My Life (continued)

Victoria Q. Walton

As I reflect on my life when I was a child, my beautiful mother, **Victoria Q. Walton**, who was a professional cook, taught me everything about cooking. When I became an adult, my family enjoyed every meal prepared for them. Mom was my inspiration throughout my life. As a child, I would not go to bed until I completed all of my homework. My mom only had a fourth-grade education, but I believed that my mom could do anything. When I needed help with my homework, mom sought help from others, even after midnight. She would say, "Help me because she is not going to bed." Mom was the fabric of my life.

Another fabric I possess is seeing my deceased sister and brother's children and grandchildren grow up as gifted and talented individuals. Each of them had struggles in life but God's providential and sovereign power have moved them from one degree of grace to another. The following are my brother, **Hillary Walton's**, children.

- **Carlton Walton, Sr.** was ordained as a minister of the Gospel, November 4, 2018. On May 3, 2019, he transferred to eternal rest.
- **Jasper Walton**, a jack-of-all-trades as a clothing designer, maintenance technician, and builder.
- **Victoria Porter**, a Florence Nightingale for Social Services, takes care of children.
- **Verna Bowden**, is a person who helps "The Least of These" out of her resources.
- **Latonya Walton**, great-niece and daughter of Verna, is an educator in the school system of Chatham County, Georgia, selected "Teacher of the Year for 2018."

- **Edna Walton Dailey**, my deceased brother, Hillary's wife, is a role model for their children. She is ninety-six years old with beauty, charm, and intelligence.
- My deceased sister, **Delores Holley**, was a fabric of my life. She was a role model as a mother and provider. From 1954 to 1958, she was employed with AT&T Technologies (Western Electric) in Kearny, New Jersey as a writer and assembler. From 1985 to 1991 she was employed as a wire specialist for ITT Avionics and from 1991 until retirement in 1997, she was employed as an instrument assembler for the Kearfott Guidance and Navigation Corporation. During her nearly forty-year career in telecommunications, Delores received several safety awards and citations for perfect attendance.
- **Vanessa Holley**, Delores' daughter and my niece, is a retired, gifted artist.
- **Erica Holley Martin,** Vanessa's daughter, a graduate of Howard University, Washington, D.C. with a degree in communications, was once known as "Erica Kane" radio announcer in the Washington, D.C. and Baltimore area.
- **Isabella**, Erica's daughter, is a gifted student.
- **Martina Holley**, my sister's grandchild and my grand-niece, is in the theatrical world in California. Her deceased father and my nephew, **Marcella Holley,** was a fabric in my life that reflected on God's guidance and faith that God provides for us.

- **Anthony "Tony" Holley**, my sister's son and my nephew, was once a slave to Satan, but now he is a follower of Christ.
  Psalms 100:3 (NIV) tells us, "Know that the Lord is God. It is he who made us, and we are his; we are his people, the sheep of his pasture."
- **Michael Holley**, my sister's youngest child and my nephew is deceased. He served in the Navy and was honorably discharged due to injuries.
- My deceased brother, **Edwin Harris**, was a star in my crown. When I was attending Teachers College Columbia University, New York, New York for my master's degree in elementary school administration, he typed my research papers and looked after me for four summers. I was very proud of my brother because he was an engineer and he tested first place when he had to take the New Jersey State test.

Father God, at eighty-eight years old, I praise you for giving me life with my family and friends. We are never alone in the world; therefore, we depend on others for more than just mere survival.

Interdenominational Ministers' Wives and Ministers' Widows Alliance of Tidewater

To my sisters of the Interdenominational Ministers' Wives and Ministers' Widows Alliance of Tidewater, the fabric that you sowed in my life throughout the years was how you enriched my life in a way directed by God. I'm grateful to people like you who put happiness into action.

On February 6, 2006, you celebrated me as the "Minister Wife of the Year."

Good friends are hard to find, harder to leave, and impossible to forget. You are a fabric in my life.

Iota Omega Chapter of Alpha Kappa Alpha Sorority, Inc.

To my sorority sisters of Iota Omega Chapter of Alpha Kappa Alpha Sorority, Inc., you are a piece of fabric that has many interwoven threads woven in my life such as creative unity, trust and bond together.

Throughout the years, you have bestowed upon me the following honors:

- Soror of the Year Award, 2004-2005
- Vivian Carter Mason Award for Outstanding Community Service, 2003
- The Eula Edmonds Glover Award for Volunteer Community Service by the 49th Mid-Atlantic Regional Conference, Alpha Kappa Alpha Sorority, Inc., 2002
- The Unsung Hero Award by Iota Omega Chapter of Alpha Sorority (Pan Hellenic Council), 1993
- The Arlene Black Award, 2010

Threads In My Life

When my husband became pastor of Warren Grove Missionary Baptist Church in 1978, my mother, Mrs. Victoria Queenie Walton, donated fifty-dollars to start a scholarship program. William Privott received the first scholarship for $100 in 1979.

Thereafter, in 2005, **The Doretha-Hall Thomas Scholarship** was established by her husband, the late Josiah Thomas, who donated $10,000 after his wife's death. **Shirley Hall and her husband, the late John Hall,** and the Thomas families continued this effort and each year on Christian Education Day they presented from $6,000 to $8,000 to the Doretha-Hall Thomas Scholarship fund.

This thread in my life lets me know that with Christ, we can do all things who strengthens us (Phil. 4:13).

Carlton Griffin

Carlton Griffin, your thread in my life consists of your decision to increase the Warren Grove Missionary Baptist Church Scholarship from $750 to $1500 each year out of your resources. God bless you for your faithfulness and generosity.

The words of Thomas Carlyle tell us that, "Everywhere in life the true question is, not what we have gained, but what we do."

The Fabric Of Life
Ella Spates Fauntleroy

Ella Spates Fauntleroy, you are a thread in my crown because you participated in the Christian Education Scholarship Program that God directed me to develop as First Lady at Warren Grove Missionary Baptist Church in Edenton, North Carolina when my husband was pastor.

The thread that you have sown in my life is your generosity as a giver to the scholarship program. The scholarship in your mother's name, Roxie Roberts Scholarship, for a student eligible to receive a $1,000 scholarship each year based on criteria. Your generosity was a lifestyle cultivated and directed by God. You are a piece of fabric that touched my life.

Frances Powell

Frances Powell, you and your late husband, James Powell (my cousin), gave gifts to Warren Grove Missionary Baptist Church, when my husband was pastor. You not only gave gifts but you directed our path to contact Mr. West Byrum to sell us land next to our educational building to build a dining hall.

When we contacted Mr. Byrum, he gave us the land. The chandeliers in the dining hall you gave out of love. A generous giver models the joy of giving, "...It is more blessed to give than to receive" (Acts 20:35).

You will always be a fabric in my life.

James White

James White, you provided a thread in my life when I asked you to update the display in the educational building about the history of the Christian Education Scholarship Program, after the retirement of my husband, Reverend Wilbert Mills, Sr. May God bless you for your faithfulness.

Mary White

Mary White, you and your brother-in-law, **Deacon Percy White**, sowed threads in my life when I was first lady that are still lingering in my life.

When I presented workshops at the Baptist Association and conferences, you made sure that the church and the community were aware of them and how God blessed me as a presenter.

Your thread in my life strengthened my belief that life is a place of service and in that service, one experiences a great deal of joy. Thank you for your faithfulness.

Reverend and Mrs. Bernard Hurdle

Reverend Bernard Hurdle and your wife, Sister Doris Hurdle, are threads in my life that will last forever. You were encouragers, supporters, and participants of all programs and ministries that God directed me to fulfill as first lady. Even today, you keep the fire burning in my life by your frequent phone calls. I will always cherish your thoughtfulness.

Mrs. Arvilla Bonner Warren

Mrs. Arvilla Bonner Warren, your thread in my life is wrapped around the word "love". You brighten up my life in your words and actions. This thread lingers in my heart with a melody of love.

Mrs. Alice Bonner

Mrs. Alice Bonner, you and your daughter, Sadie Bonner, are threads you have sown in my life and my husband's life when you prepared dinners for us on Sundays after services. You have our heartfelt thanks for all that you've done. Your service is measured by sincerity and integrity. Thank God for the fabric of life and love.

God has also blessed me with the following people in my life.

Mrs. Patricia Sims

Mrs. Patricia Sims, the fabric you have sown in my life started in 1986 and it is still in operation. When I was the principal of Suburban Park Elementary School in Norfolk, Virginia, you were one of the parents who was involved in the school's parental involvement programs. You worked with the teachers and me as a goal setter for your children's education. I cherish your thread in my life as we continue to talk about the success of your children who are now adults.

Kenneth Fuller, Jay Towler, William Lyons and Marcus Cotton

Kenneth Fuller, Jay Towler, William Lyons, and Marcus Cotton, you are the keys that start my teaching session on the fifth Sunday to one of the adult classes by setting up my teaching display charts. Your custodial/ administrative staff is a thread and fabric in my life because you follow through with my needs. The People's Community Baptist Church under the pastoral ministry of Reverend Dr. Haywood Robinson, III is blessed by the service you render.

Germaine Leftridge

Germaine, you are a star in my crown,
Love to have you around,
To lift up my spirit, with what you say.
Keep on doing it your way.

You make me feel upbeat and sublime.
Please don't stop because I feel young at heart each and
every time.

I shall never forget you as I stroll down memory lane each
and every day.
Thank you Germaine for doing it your way!

You are a fabric in my life.

Germaine,

I have faith to believe that you are a Business Queen, who works your heart out with a gleam.

You are a stalwart woman of God because you are characterized by firmness, determination, and adventurous motives.

Always on task, but looks to God and asks,

"Lord, will You lead me and guide me along the way?

Give me Your Spirit to never sway from serving You and others each and every day."

You display a life that is forceful, strong, and enduring, even when life is hard to climb.

God's grace and mercy restore your soul to be compassionate toward others.

Germaine, you are a stalwart woman!

Dr. Susie M. Hill

Dr. Susie M. Hill, I shall always remember your teachings about the Modesty of Women. You taught as a stalwart woman of God. Through surges of God's power you possess under His guidance, you find happiness. Special gifts God has breathed on your life, despite circumstances; you always suffice to celebrate your beliefs on life for women.

Starr McCray

Starr McCray, I shall always remember you as an extended daughter. In 2005, my husband invited 250 people to a Gala Banquet at Grand Affairs in Virginia Beach, Virginia to celebrate my life. You decorated the Grand Affairs Ballroom with crystal lights, flowers on each table, and throughout the room. The head table was a beautiful décor. I cherish your life in my life. I also remember when my husband and I celebrated our twenty-fifth wedding anniversary. You sent us to the Lighthouse on the water in Smithfield, Virginia. You left your credit card with the manager in case we needed anything else.

You are still a star in my crown and a fabric in my life.

Donna Stephens

Donna Stephens, the fabrics you have sown in my life are faithful friendship, loyalty, and service to others. You give real service as Administrator Director of the Lions Medical Eye Bank & Research Center of Eastern Virginia. You were responsible for my husband and me to serve on the Advisory Council in Norfolk, Virginia.

At our monthly meetings and annual luncheons organized by you and your staff, the testimonies inspired me about life.

A cornea transplant is a surgical procedure to replace part of your cornea with cornea tissue from a donor. A donor transplant can restore vision, reduce pain and improve the appearance of a damaged or diseased cornea. When I was president of my community civic league, our involvement with the Eye Bank, and information received was transferred to the residents in our community. Thank you, Donna, for your service to mankind.

Dr. Beverly Harris and Reverend Dr. Stephen Harris

To Dr. Beverly Harris and Reverend Dr. Stephen Harris, you are threads sown in my life that's woven in love, dedication, and sacrifice. Both of you sacrificed fifteen years of dedicated service as workshop leaders at our Annual Church-Wide Institute, which was developed and organized in 1978 when my husband became pastor of Warren Grove Missionary Baptist Church located in Edenton, North Carolina. The Church-Wide Institute was held each year, the last weekend in March. Your workshop titles included, "Strengthening Your Marriage," "Stewardship: Managing Your Time, Talent and Money," "Managing Healthy Lifestyles," "Managing Your Finances Is A Spiritual Challenge," "Developing Strategies For Spiritual Warfare," to name just a few. We selected you and Reverend Dr. Harris because of your dedicated service at the Virginia State Baptist Convention under Dr. Lois Brown, Director, who served for twenty-five years. God also blessed me to serve as Assistant Director in charge of the Search Sessions Workshops at the Convention. Dr. Beverly Harris, you were in charge of the women ministry sessions and Reverend Dr. Stephen Harris headed the brotherhood sessions. Both of you made the ultimate sacrifice in time and resources in service to others. With this background, your giving not getting, brought us real happiness at Warren Grove. Thank God for your service to mankind. Your thread of service is still in my heart.

Dr. Beverly Harris, your records show that you received the Doctor of Education from Nova Southeastern University, Fort Lauderdale, Florida, June 2019. Reverend Dr. Stephen Harris, you received your Doctor of Ministry from the University of Lynchburg, Lynchburg, Virginia in 2009.

A beacon light will always shine in my life of your service to mankind.

Dr. Olivia Newby and Dr. James Newby, M.D.

To Dr. Olivia Newby and Dr. James Newby, M.D., you are the charming gardeners who make a life blossom. I shall always remember November 27, 2016, when you enriched my husband's and my life with a great celebration before we relocated to Maryland. Olivia, your fabric in my life is when you were my Sunday school teacher and your teaching of Christ and the Word of God.

A Fabric of Life To Remember: Appointment to the Virginia Beach Human Rights Commission

I was appointed to the Virginia Beach Human Rights Commission in 1981. **City Councilman, Louis Jones,** recommended me to this position. During my tenure as a Human Rights Commissioner, I also served as vice-chair.

This fabric of my life as a Commissioner consisted of diversity to the social fabric of the city. Visitations to the city's Juvenile Detention Home were an opportunity to review the services and atmosphere of the facility for juveniles and the rehabilitation activities/ programs.

This position also required knowledge of the social fabric of intolerance in the city of everyday life.

Thank you, Councilman Jones, for believing in me.

This Thread Will Linger

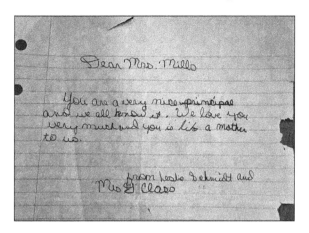

Handwritten letter from student 1983

This thread will linger in my heart forever. God blessed me to find this one by Leslie. I think it was written around 1983 when I became the principal of my first school, Roberts Park Elementary School, which was an inner-city school located in the project of Roberts Park in Norfolk, Virginia.

God blessed me to organize an acceleration program during the summer for four weeks to uplift and enrich the students' performance in reading, math, and test-taking skills. The school administration and research department approved the program and provided transportation to the school. Because of the improved test scores after the program, the research department recommended a second year of the program.

Norfolk State University Testing Department conducted test-taking sessions.

Also, teachers on my staff and in the community conducted the teaching sessions.

Mary Jane Bakery provided snacks for the children.

My cafeteria staff and parents organized the snack period.

Thank you, Leslie. I'm glad that I found your thoughts on life.

Remembering a Fabric In My Life
Marvin Bonner

When my husband became pastor of Warren Grove Missionary Baptist Church in Edenton, North Carolina in 1978, God blessed me to tutor Marvin Bonner, who was a fourth-grader at that time. Marvin had a speech disorder that resulted in stuttering. I worked with Marvin for four years using a phonetic program, "Let's Make It Difficult For Children To Fail." I purchased the program from Mrs. Ruth Qualls, one of the founders of the program, when I was the principal of an inner-city school.

After using the program, Marvin was a shining star when the youth of the church had to recite Bible verses during the youth worship period. Marvin would recite ten or more verses at one time.

Marvin Bonner graduated from North Carolina State University in 2011 with a B.S. degree in Food Safety. On May 5, 2019, he received a Master of Science degree from Michigan State University in food safety.

Marvin has been promoted as a food inspector, and in 2020 he will move to Orlando, Florida.

I shall always remember this fabric in my life.

I was presented with the Excellence Award by "Let's Make It Difficult For Children to Fail" on September 4, 1991.

Conclusions

This chapter portrays some examples of how people can make a difference in a person's life. The fabrics and threads that were produced in my life portrayed courage, love, faith, and determination with God's help.

The American Heritage Dictionary gives the following as a definition of tapestry. Tapestry: A heavy cloth woven with rich, often varicolored designs or scenes, usually hung on walls for decoration and sometimes used to cover furniture.[11] The tapestry of life is similar. We begin to see our designs from a wider angle of years. When we weave the tapestries of our lives from year to year, we need to look to God for guidance because God is our rock in a weary land. He designs our divine gifts, unique talents, thoughts, choices, and actions. The fabric of human life can be made brand new by obedience to God's commands.

A damaged fabric cannot be made brand new by a patch or re-weaving.

Yet with our life woven together by the wondrous hands of the Creator, we can make a difference. Galatians 2:20 (ESV) states, "I have been crucified with Christ. It is no longer I who live, but Christ who lives in me and gave himself for me..."

Jeremiah 29:11 (ESV) states, "For I know the plans I have for you, declares the Lord, plans for welfare and not for evil, to give you a future and a hope."

Thank you, God, for all the threads and fabrics that have been sown in my life. The shape of my life started when I was baptized at nine years old. I grew up listening to saints using language to live *in grace* as much of the time as possible. By grace, meant an inner harmony, essentially spiritual, which can be translated into outward harmony.

Let me end with the thought, "Believe that life is worth living when God directs your path."

A Life Changed by Grace

God's grace is so amazing because His grace is free and because we do not deserve it. Paul writes in 2 Corinthians 9:8, "And God is able to make all grace abound toward you; that ye, always having all sufficiency in all things, may abound to every good work:"

We are given grace to repent, grace to believe, grace to be saved. We are given grace to understand the Word of God. We are given grace to defeat temptation. We are given grace to endure suffering, disappointment, and pain. We are given grace to obey the Lord. We are given grace to serve Him by using our spiritual gifts, which are gifts of grace. This great grace is received through obedient faith.

God's grace is a person. Jesus Christ is God's grace personified.

Many of us believe that we have to change, grow, and be good in order to be loved. But rather we are loved and we receive His grace so we can change, grow, and be good.

God's grace gives us the freedom to face God and face the truth about us in the light of God's Word. Knowing we are fully loved and accepted by Him, He calls us to come to Him with everything so that He can help us experience freedom (John 8:32) and a more abundant life (John 10:10).

Marital unfaithfulness is one of those events that cause deep inner pain. Sometimes the marriage may never be restored. But even then we can demonstrate God's grace through forgiveness.

Because of God's grace, you no longer need to compare yourself to others or feel God has blessed them more.

God's grace is powerful. It's life-changing, and it's so much like Jesus. God laid down Jesus's life for our sins and gave us His all.

"'...God opposes the proud but gives grace to the humble.'" (1 Peter 5:5 NLT). "Humble yourselves therefore under the mighty hand of God, that he may exalt you in due time: Casting all your care upon him; for he careth for you" (1 Pet. 5:6-7).

If we want to experience God's grace, we need to come in truth and humility. James 4:6 (NLT) says, "...God opposes the proud but He gives grace to the humble."

Grace is not something simply to be claimed, it is to be demonstrated. Hebrews 4:16 says, "Let us therefore come boldly unto the throne of grace, that we may obtain mercy, and find grace to help in time of need."

St. Paul knew God's grace as he changed from a life of violence and persecuting Christians to a life of preaching the gospel. Faith may have come to St. Paul in the form of being knocked off a horse and given a vision of Christ, but he was blinded. He spent years in the wilderness cultivating his relationship with God. He was persecuted just as he had persecuted.

It wasn't easy for St. Paul to preach the gospel, but by God's grace, he did.

Because of God's grace, you no longer have to strive in self-sufficiency because His grace enables you to do what you cannot do on your own (2 Cor. 12:8-9). Through God's empowering grace, you can love others well. Through grace, you are freed from feeling that you have to hide your sin from Him. God's grace enables you to be all He has called you to be.

Because of grace, you no longer need to compare yourself to others or feel God has blessed them more. You no longer need to live in shame. God's grace isn't a church phrase that has no substance. It's powerful. It's life-changing, and it's so much like Jesus.

Our prayer each day should be a prayer praising God for His life-changing grace. Ask for help to believe His gift of grace more and more each day.

On Becoming As An Educator

*I*n 1985, I attended a principals' conference where Dr. Leo Buscaglia was the motivational speaker. His warm presentation inspired me because he talked about teaching all children, the quiet ones, the withdrawn ones, the non-verbal child, the orderly, and the intelligent and serene child, which touched my heart. My background in child development and as a psycho-educational specialist gave me greater knowledge and understanding about children.

Dr. Buscaglia described his personal experience of being labeled as retarded due to a language barrier in his early years. He was born in Los Angeles, but his immigrant family moved to Italy right after his birth. He was fluent in Italian after living in an Italian village for about five years. After returning to Los Angeles, he did not speak English and this is why he was moved to a class with retarded children. Fortunately, a wonderful teacher who nurtured him and showed him love, worked to have him placed in a regular class. Can you imagine the impact this had on his young life?

During that conference in 1985, Dr. Leo Buscaglia's presentation stressed love and the power of touch, especially through hugging. He left the participants inspired to love better, live better, and bring hope to the least among us.

On Becoming
(A Christian's View)

On becoming from a Christian's view, one must build up their character by becoming a more faithful, patient, fortified, and charitable child of God. It is through sorrow and suffering, toil and tribulation that one gains the education, which makes one more like God's saints in heaven.

Hebrews 5:8 states that one must be obedient and learn from the things which one suffers from. One must put their trust in the Lord.

On becoming, let others see that you are going forward for God in your life and you are doing it through the strength of the Spirit of God.

On becoming, every Christian should expect some suffering. We should realize that it is part of life according to the Word of God.

1 Peter 4:12 says, "Beloved, think it not strange concerning the fiery trial which is to try you, as though some strange thing happened unto you."

The Word is telling us that suffering is for the faith of Jesus Christ. Suffering was common for the early Christians. The early Christians suffered for their faith in Jesus Christ. Jesus suffered and therefore understands our sorrows. He has been there and has felt our pain. He came to earth and became a man that He might understand and have compassion. Rather than try to kill our pain with sedatives, we need to turn to our compassionate Savior to bear our pain and suffering.

Stalwart Men and Women of God

The men and women described in this chapter make their life a masterpiece because they live what they teach and they walk what they talk.

Each acrostic writing tells a story about living and giving service to mankind. Galatians 5:13-14 states, "For, brethren, ye have been called unto liberty; only use not liberty for an occasion to the flesh, but by love serve one another. For all the law is fulfilled in one word, even in this; Thou shalt love thy neighbor as thyself."

Each person in this chapter has an aim in life and it is victory. God wants us to be victorious. He wants us to triumph over all our foes. Stalwart and brave we must stand. God is at the helm. There is no reason for defeat.

The men and women in this chapter are true to their God-given callings and their gifts. They love God with all their heart, soul, mind, and strength. They love their fellow persons as themselves. That's why they are stalwart men and women of God.

A Stalwart Pastor of God

Dr. Haywood A. Robinson, III

H   Reverend Dr. Haywood A. Robinson, III, as Pastor of The People's Community Baptist Church in Silver Spring, Maryland, you have a heart to carry out whatever the tide. You are always available to your parishioners

A   as you journey with God.

Y   You never walk alone because the Holy Spirit is your guide.

W   Wisdom from God makes your life sublime.

O   Only God moves you from one degree of grace to another all the time.

O   On the shoulder of God, you have a deeper view.

D   Down in your heart you promote life, by reaching out to others and doing it God's way.

R   Romans 8:28 says, "And we know that all things work together for good to them that love God, to them who are called according to his purpose."

O   Only God provides a life for you to suffice. You demonstrate the words of Proverbs 27:23-24,

B   "Be though diligent to know the state of thy flocks, and look well in thy herds. For riches are not forever: and doth the crown endure to every generation?"
Your core mission of your church is to make and mobilize disciples who will advance the kingdom of God. Thank God, Pastor for your faithfulness.

I   In faith, you move forward with God letting Him use you for His kingdom and His glory. Pastor Robinson, your shepherd's

N   nature demonstrates love and care for your flock because you have a

S   strong ability to empathize with a hurting person.

O   On the shoulders of God, you are a peacemaker. We

N   need you because of your fervent and thriving relationship with God. Our worship services prepare the saints for the work of service, to build up the body of Christ.

Reverend Dr. Haywood Robinson, III, you are truly a stalwart Pastor of God. You demonstrate what Acts 20:28 says, "Take heed therefore unto yourselves, and to all the flock, over which the Holy Ghost hath made you overseers, to feed the church of God, which he hath purchased with his own blood."

Also, 2 Timothy 4:2 (NIV) says. "Preach the word; be prepared in season and out of season, correct, rebuke and encourage--with great patience and careful in instruction."

Pastor Robinson, your life and ministry preparation includes studies at Hampton Institute (now Hampton University), Capital Bible Seminary, a Master of Divinity degree, and at Howard University School of Divinity, a doctorate degree in ministry.

Pastor, your stalwart work and service in the community has been recognized in various ways. Among them was your induction into the prestigious Martin Luther King Jr. Board of Preachers at Morehouse College, Atlanta, Georgia. Over the years, you have served Christ as an evangelist, counselor, psalmist, teacher, and in many other capacities. You also served as president of the Minster's Conference.

In 2005, you were called to shepherd The People's Community Baptist Church, Silver Spring, Maryland, succeeding the founder, the Reverend Dr. Thomas J. Baltimore, Sr.

Thank God for you, Pastor. You are a blessing to our church. Your sermons are relatable, practical, that help one walk out of church with the tools and motivation for a better life.

The records show that your ministerial life began as a teenager under the pastoral ministry of your father, Dr. Haywood Robinson, Jr. God touched your life as a teenager and even after a brief career as a public school educator; you answered God's call to the Gospel Ministry. You were licensed and ordained at the Round Oak Missionary Baptist Church in Silver Spring, Maryland.

Pastor Robinson, life is all about going upward and downward to pursue our dreams. You did not let any kind of obstacle and failure pin you down or push you against your successful life. You took the challenges with courage, determination, and perseverance.

Pastor Robinson, you and first lady Renee are blessed with three adult children, Andre, Jacqueline, Jordan, two grandchildren, Peyton and Ayanna. Praise God for your family.

Thank you for your service to mankind, God's way.

A Stalwart Woman of God

First Lady Renee Robinson

R   Renee, you are very special at The People's Community Baptist Church as first lady. It is also

E   evident that you are a mother, grandmother, and the wife of a man of God, Reverend Dr. Haywood Robinson, III.

N   Nothing separates your love from him and your family

E   even in the darkest moments when your husband needs to vent, you are an

E   encourager as stated in Philippians 4:8, "Finally brethren, whatsoever things are true, whatsoever things are honest, whatsoever things are just, whatsoever things are pure, whatsoever things are lovely, whatsoever things are of good reports; if there be any virtue, and if there be any praise, think on these things."

R   Renee, there is no cookie-cutter approach on the actual role of the pastor's wife. However,

O   one of your truly remarkable qualities is when you show a faithful love for the members you serve as you teach the new members class. As first lady, you have also placed

B   balance in your role as first lady. This is very important because you focus on your family life, Christ, and His bride, the church.

I   In your role, I believe you pray for your husband every day that God will place guardian angels around your husband, protecting him against all evil or hindrances that may cause harm or problems for him. Mark 9:29 tells us that some things are only accomplished through prayer and fasting. You also go beyond the

N   normal by being

S   supportive with strength when your husband needs someone to lean on.

O   Only God can fulfill a first lady's role. You

N   never give up but always seek God's plan.

First lady Renee Robinson, you are a stalwart woman of God with compassion to support your husband. When God calls a man into the ministry, He calls the whole man and that includes his wife and the whole family. May God bless you in your role as first lady.

Postscript

Records show that you graduated from Hampton Institute, now Hampton University.

A Stalwart Pastor of God

Pastor Calvin N. Baltimore, Emeritus

C   Reverend Dr. Calvin N. Baltimore, Emeritus throughout the years you have fulfilled an incredible amount of ministry responsibilities. God

A   allowed you to be a vessel to train ministers of the Gospel. Your

L   labor was not in

V   vain. The president of Madison University was

I   inspired by your efforts of training ministers. This spiritual discipline is the strict training that Paul was talking about in 1 Corinthians 9:25 which says, "And every man that striveth for the mastery is temperate in all things. Now they do it to obtain a corruptible crown, but we are incorruptible." Pastor Baltimore, throughout your life as a minister and pastor, you persevered and

N   never gave up without seeking help from God to accomplish great things. Your background shows throughout your life as a minister and pastor. You labored diligently to bring under your wings to teach God's Word to those entrusted in your care. Psalms 37:28 (MSG) states, "... God loves this kind of thing, never turns away from his friends. Live this way and you've got it made, but bad eggs will be tossed out." We

N   never get too much of God's truth. The truth is always found outside of us and only in Christ. Your background shows that throughout your life as a minister and pastor, you labored diligently to teach about studying the

B   Bible.

A   As a stalwart pastor throughout the years, you laid down the proclamation of the Word of God. This duty is

L   listed in Jeremiah 3:15, "And I will give you pastors according to mine heart, which shall feed you with knowledge and understanding." You also demonstrated

T   the duties of a pastor in your teaching about Jesus Christ.

I   Isaiah 40:11 says, "He shall feed his flock like a shepherd: he shall gather the lambs with his arm, and carry them in his bosom, and shall gently lead those that are with young." God blessed you to

M   model Christ in His love for the church so that the church be inspired to follow His leadership and be like Christ.

O   Only God moved you from one degree of grace to another. As you

R   reached out to others, you inspired them to love Christ and love one another.

Psalms 37:27 (MSG) says, "Turn your back on

E   evil, work for the good, and don't quit."

Reverend Dr. Calvin Baltimore, you are a stalwart man of God. April 20, 2019, marked your forty-sixth year in the ministry. You have pastored three churches, Third Zion Baptist Church, Front Royal, Virginia, Poplar Forks Baptist Church, Warrenton, Virginia, and First Baptist Church of Harrisonburg, Virginia, twelve years retired Pastor Emeritus. You were instrumental in helping your brother, founder, the late Reverend T.J. Baltimore, in organizing The People's Community Baptist Church in Silver Spring, Maryland. You received a B.A. degree in Business Administration in 1964 from Virginia State College in Petersburg, Virginia now Virginia State University, and a master's degree in business administration from Strayer University. You attended Washington Bible College in 1976-1979 and received a Certificate in Biblical Studies.

In 1984, you received the Doctor of Ministry at Shaw University, Raleigh, North Carolina. Pastor Baltimore, you have been a member of the National Capital Baptist

Convention, Washington, D.C. for twelve years. In 2018, you assumed the presidency of the Evangelism Board. You are also a member of the National Baptist USA Evangelism Board and a member of the National Ketoctan Baptist Association and Dean of Second National Ketoctan Baptist Association.

For a total of twenty-six years, you served under Reverend T.J. Baltimore and Reverend Dr. Haywood Robinson, III as an associate minister.

God has blessed you with a son and four grandchildren. They live in Maryland. Thank you for all that you have done for God and what He has done for you.

Remembering A Stalwart Woman of God

Deaconess Barbara Bolden

When Deaconess Barbara Bolden was on earth and before God called her to her heavenly home, she was

B   Bold with God's love,

A   always ready to move with directions from above.

R   Reaching out to others with God's love and advice, she

B   brought out the best in people

A   as a disciple of Christ. Barbara Bolden

R   recognized God's amazing grace because grace

A   allowed her to say, each and every day, that the

B   best of life is when you do it God's way. Deaconess Barbara Bolden had wonderful thoughts

O   on life, such as "When

L   life's challenges and sorrows come your way, you

D   do not stop;

E   even in your darkest moments and whatever the tide, your faith lets you know that

N   new life will be given by God, and you will survive."

Deaconess Barbara Bolden was a stalwart woman of God. The life that she created was meaningful. Before her death, she called me and wanted to know if I had the decorative Washington, D.C. towels and the twenty-four karat gold-plated writing pen that she had given me for my birthday in April 2018.

During this period, Sister Barbara was under a specific study at Johns Hopkins Hospital. The week before she passed, she called and requested prayer. She did not let me know that her life was ending. However, since she is in her heavenly home, she still exists in many of our lives, because the life she created in our hearts will never stop beating.

So long Deaconess Barbara, until we meet again.

Postscript

Deaconess Bolden was hired by the United States Federal Government in 1967. She moved from one degree of grace to another by furthering her career in education. She earned a B.S. degree in Business Administration from the University of the District of Columbia, in Washington, D.C. Deaconess Bolden worked directly with Dr. Roderick R. Paige, former cabinet member, and the first African American Secretary of the U.S. Department of Education under President George W. Bush, as his confidential special assistant, and supervisor for the Front Office of the Secretary.

Deaconess Bolden was a faithful servant of The People's Community Baptist Church in Silver Spring, Maryland, under the leadership of Reverend Dr. Haywood Robinson, III. She served as a deaconess and was involved in the prayer ministry, where she was a moderator on the prayer line.

Deaconess Bolden departed this life on Tuesday, September 4, 2018, at her home in Silver Spring, Maryland. She is survived by her husband, James Melvin Bolden. God blessed them to adopt their thirteen-year-old great-nephew, Jelani Melvin Ruffin.

A Stalwart Woman of God

Thelma Bowes

T   Thelma Bowes, you are like a, "...nail in a sure place..." (Isa. 22:23), as a manager of a credit union.

H   Helping others is what you do each and every day.

E   Encouraging people when they are in need financially.

L   Like a bridge over troubled waters, you respond to their request in a timely manner. God has given you the grace to

M   meet your customer's needs. It's God's

A   amazing grace when you reach out to others.

B   Beyond your job as a Federal Credit Union Manager, you help serve Thanksgiving dinner to homeless families. This is an

O   Outreach Ministry at St. Martin Church in Washington, D.C. This is an opportune time to sit with families and talk about God. For James 2:14-16 tells us,
What doth it profit, my brethren, though a man say he hath faith, and have not works? can faith save him?
If a brother or a sister be naked, and destitute of daily food, And one of you say unto them, Depart in peace, be ye warmed and filled; notwithstanding ye give them not those things which are needful to the body; what doth it profit?

W   Words in your heart give you patience and understanding when you deal with people. You also give

E   endurance by identifying customers needs and suggest a solution that will improve their financial life. You

S   sacrifice your time to help others.

Thelma Bowes, you are a stalwart woman of God.

You lead to help people glorify God. You are like a light on a hill that shines before others, so that they may see your good works and give glory to your Father who is in heaven. When you participate in the Outreach Ministry at St. Martin's Church on Thanksgiving Day, you serve the families and teach the Word of God. You are an excellent example of the meaning of life, love, and service.

God blessed you to graduate from Bishop College, Dallas, Texas with a B.S. degree in Marketing Management. You have two children, Claudia, age eighteen, who is a freshman at Penn

State University and a son, Gerard, age twenty-three, who is a graduate from Frostburg University, Maryland.

Thank you for all that you do and your service to mankind.

A Stalwart Woman of God

Cora Bridgers

C   Cora, you have always been a, "...nail in a sure place..." (Isa. 22:23), thinking of

O   others and guiding them under the directions of God. When you were a teacher of the gifted and talented program in Norfolk, Virginia you took

R   risks that supported the gifted child's success.

A   Activities that you provided caused them to be

B   bold to

R   reach their potentials

I   in the learning process. You taught the gifted learners to

D   demand to be stretched and to

G   grow daily with one's self and envision schooling as an

E escalator on which students continually progress, rather than a series of stairs, with landings on which advanced learners consistently wait.

R Responsive instruction you provided indicated growth and

S success.

Cora Bridgers, you are a stalwart woman of God with zeal and success.

Postscript

My husband and I shall always remember you as our daughter, Andrea's, Sunday school teacher when she was five years old. Each night before she went to bed, she was on her knees reading the Bible and praying.

I told my husband what I had observed each night when I passed Andrea's room. I asked him if he told Andrea to do that. He replied, "I thought you did." When we asked Andrea why she read her Bible each night and prayed, she said, "Mrs. Bridgers told me to do it."

Today, Andrea is still reading her Bible and praying before she goes to bed.

Proverbs 22:6 (KJV) tells us to, "Train up a child in the way he should go: and when he is old, he will not depart from it." Thank you, Mrs. Bridgers, for being a teacher and a servant of God.

Your records show that you graduated from North Carolina A&T University, Greensboro, North Carolina with a Bachelor of Science degree. You also attended Norfolk State University. God blessed you to receive certification in gifted education from William and Mary University in Williamsburg, Virginia and Old Dominion University, Norfolk, Virginia. You retired after thirty-four and a half years with Norfolk Public Schools.

Sister Bridgers, your life has always been a place of service with a great deal of joy, for fifty-four years as a Sunday school teacher to the teenagers and children at Second Calvary Baptist Church in Norfolk, Virginia. God has also blessed you in your leadership with the NAACP Membership Drive and NAACP Freedom Banquet for over thirty years.

Your life journey has been a mixture of sunshine and rain. Being a survivor of breast and lung cancer since 1994, you are an active member of the Cancer Research Committee at Second Calvary Baptist Church. Under the order of God's beauty, you did not fear life, you let Him guide you and order your steps as He orders the stars. God gave you inner peace.

You were born and educated in Tillery, North Carolina. God has blessed you with three sons, Roderick, Aaron, Patrick, and one daughter, Vanessa Bridgers Boone. You are blessed with the following grandchildren: Ian Edmond Bridgers, Aaron Patrick Bridgers, and Hunter Patrick Bridgers.

Sister Bridgers, your life has been courageous.

You believe that life is worth living. The Word in Joshua 1:9 (KJV) says, "...Be strong and of a good courage; be not afraid, neither be thou dismayed: for the Lord thy God is with thee whithersoever thou goest."

A Stalwart Woman of God

Trumillia Britt

T   Trumillia Britt you are a stalwart woman of God who lives a life for others, as a mother, church member, and an educator. You were an outstanding caregiver to your husband until his death.

"The

R   righteous person may have many troubles, but the Lord delivers him from them all" (Ps. 34:19 NIV).

You are always ready to move because God

U   understands your plight.

M   Many days you reach out

I   in an unknown land to

L   lift up other's spirits to live, and

L   love

I   in sunshine or rain. Proverbs 17:17 (NIV) tells us,

A   "A friend loves at all times, and a brother is born for a time of adversity." Trumillia, you also

B   bear the fruit of the Holy Spirit. Paul wrote, "...the fruit of the Spirit is love, joy, peace, longsuffering, gentleness, goodness, faith, meekness, temperance..." (Galatians 5:22-23). Trumillia, life is about the way one wants to be

R   remembered. You are mostly admired by others because of your

I   integrity and loyalty. You have taught many people and especially the students that you taught as an educator. You stressed, don't let bad

T   thoughts make a home in your mind because they will steal your joy. I witnessed how you

T   trusted God as an educator, and how He gave you tremendous victory. As your principal at Suburban Park Elementary School, I witnessed your spiritual guidance as a devotional leader during faculty meetings. You also chaired our self-study assessment of the school for the Virginia State Department of Education.

Trumillia Britt, you are a stalwart woman of God, born in Enfield, North Carolina. You are a graduate of Elizabeth City State University and you received a Bachelor of Science degree in Elementary Education in 1960.

In 1980, you received a master's degree in elementary administration from the University of Virginia.

You are a devout member of New Bethel Baptist Church, Portsmouth, Virginia. You serve as a deacon, trustee, chairperson of the Missionary Ministry and the Women's Ministry.

You reach out to the community by visiting nursing homes and celebrate the birthdays of members. You commune with the sick and shut-in as a deacon. You also usher on the third Sunday.

You have received the following recognitions:

- Teacher of the Year-Award 1987-1988 for Suburban Park Elementary School and James Monroe Elementary School, 1991-1992.
- Two School Bell Awards, 1993-1994
- Featured nationally in Women's World Magazine and on TV and radio for administering a makeshift Heimlich maneuver and saving the life of one of your students who had swallowed three coins: a nickel, a dime, and a quarter.

Trumillia Britt, Galatians 6:9 (ESV) describes you, "And let us not grow weary of doing good, for in due season we will reap, if we do not give up."

You are blessed to have two gifted children. Your son, Anthony Britt, is a musician, actor, and artist. Your daughter,

Trulinda Britt, is an event planner, voice-over artist, and marketing professional.

Thank you for being a stalwart woman of God and for your service to mankind. You will always have a place in my heart and I will always have sweet memories of you as one of my best teachers.

A Stalwart Woman of God

Rilene Brookins

R   Rilene, I remember you as a teacher who possessed all the qualities of an excellent educator. In your classroom, there was

I   interaction,

L   learning, enthusiasm, and a love for the subject being taught. You also

E   engaged your students to explore activities and you adjusted to the

N   needs of your students by making material accessible to them while still challenging them to improve. You provided

E   exploratory activities each day to explore our slogan

B   "Believe, Achieve, Succeed." As an excellent teacher, you helped your students to learn and succeed with

R   resilience by reinforcing, "It's okay to be you." You
     also provided
O   opportunities for learning as you based on individual
     differences, you
O   opened the door to success, by being
K   knowledgeable of content and by giving students the
     opportunity to apply their knowledge in different ways.
I   In light of high expectations for students, you
N   nurtured and guided learning by assigning diverse
     activities. You helped many students to
S   succeed because you nurtured those students in
     your care.

Rilene Brookins, you are a stalwart woman of God. I was blessed to have you as one of my best teachers at Poplar Hall Elementary School in Norfolk, Virginia.

You have always been a successful teacher. You taught children on the elementary level at West Point Army Academy, West Point, New York Department of Defense.

You received your Bachelor of Science degree in Education from Kentucky State University, Frankfort Fort, Kentucky, and a Master of Science degree at Indiana University, Bloomington, Indiana.

God bless you for all that you have done for mankind.

Postscript

You were one of the teachers who traveled to my husband's church in Edenton, North Carolina to participate in our Saturday acceleration program for students in grades three, four, and five. The main focus was to provide direct instruction to those students who scored the lowest on the reading and math sections of the North Carolina State standards tests.

You live your life as you would climb a mountain. An occasional glance toward the summit keeps the goal in mind, but many beautiful scenes are to be observed from each new vantage point. Thanks again for your service to mankind.

Your family consists of your husband, Lionel Brookins, two adult children, Lionel III and Rochelle Brookins. God has blessed you with one granddaughter, Rheanna.

A Stalwart Man of God

Deacon Fred Brown

F   Deacon Fred Brown, God has truly blessed you with a heart of a stalwart soul. Your life has been a life on a beacon hill.

R   Resting in the arms of Jesus Christ, your Savior, and God your Father. You have lived a strong life as a steward of God and as a lawyer by profession.

You retired December 2017, after thirty-nine years as an attorney for the federal government. At the time of your retirement, you were an administrative judge and also deputy director of the Office of Hearings and Appeals of the U.S. Department of Energy. In 2008, you were appointed to the Senior Executive Service (SES) which is the highest rank attainable in the civilian federal workforce. This

E   endeavor focused on helping people in need, not just income but also educational attainment, occupational prestige, and social status.

D   Deacon Brown, your life has been sublime.

- Served as chairman of the Deacon Ministry for two years at The People's Community Baptist Church (2005 and 2006)
- Served as Tuesday Night Bible Study teacher for six years (1998-2004)
- Served in the Men's Choir for fourteen years
- Served as chairman of the Men's Fellowship for one year (1995-1996)
- Served as an adult Sunday school teacher for six years (2012 to present)
- Selected as the People's Community Baptist Church "Man of the Year" in 2012

With God beside you, He is your

B   bright and shining star among men. Galatians 6:2 (NIV) tells us to, "Carry each other's burdens, and in this way, you will fulfill the law of Christ." Deacon Fred Brown you did this when you were working because you believe the Word of

R   Romans 12:13 (NIV), "Share with the Lord's people who are in need. Practice hospitality."

O   Only God moved you from one degree of grace to another. You also demonstrated the

W   Word in Matthew 5:16, "Let your light so shine before men, that they may see your good works, and glorify your Father which is in heaven."

N   Nobody but God prepared you to receive a B.A. from Colgate University with a double major in mathematics (with honors); a law degree (Juris Doctor) from the George Washington University, National Law Center and an M.A. in Energy Policy, from George Washington University, College of General Studies.

Deacon Fred Brown, you are a stalwart man of God because God has given you the grace to lead people toward meeting the organization's vision, mission, and goals. You and your wife, Deaconess Wanda Brown, are truly stalwart persons for God with a vision to serve people in every walk of life. God bless you!

A Stalwart Woman of God

Deaconess Wanda Brown

W Deaconess Wanda Brown, you have blessed the lives of parents, children, and communities as an educator for thirty-three years. Your

A active life is renowned because as a stalwart woman, you hold a master's degree in educational psychology from Teacher's College Columbia University, New York, and a Certificate in Information Systems from George Washington University, Washington, D.C.

N Nothing stops you because your life is like the sun, it can equate happiness because it is bright. Currently you are serving in the following capacities:

- Member of the Education Committee of the National Council of Negro Women (NCNW) Potomac Valley Section (PVS)

- Member of the Montgomery County NAACP Parent's Council
- Member of the Deaconess Ministry of The People's Community Baptist Church
- Co-Chair of the Caregivers Ministry of The People's Community Baptist Church
- Chairperson of the Scholarship Committee of The People's Community Baptist Church

D   During your career as an educator for thirty-three years, you have guided children and parents.

A   According to Proverbs 22:6, "Train up a child in the way he should go: and when he is old, he will not depart from it" (Prov. 9:9). says, "Give instruction to a wise man, and he will be yet wiser: teach a just man, and he will increase in learning."

In your connection with the PVS NCNW Education Committee during the 1998 Summer Reading Challenge, two five-year-olds, read a total of seventy-two books by African American authors and Dr. Seuss books. These winners were awarded a beginner's dictionary. Nineteen years later, both of these youth graduated from prestigious universities and pursued their careers.

B   Because of your stalwart life, in 2011 you were
R   recognized by the Potomac Valley Section, National Council of Negro Women as

O   "Outstanding Member of the Year"

W   Wanda, you were honored for what you gave.

N   No matter how tough life got as you worked as an educator, you were stalwart and loyal to your allegiance.

Deaconess Wanda Brown, you are truly a stalwart woman of God with a life of faith. Throughout your life, God has guided you over all of your foes. Because you are stalwart, God has been at the helm. You are loyal and strong.

You are a native of New York. Your life in Silver Spring, Maryland with your husband, Fred, of thirty-nine years is honorable.

As stalwart people, you reflect on the following scripture in Ephesians 4:2 (NIV), "Be completely humble and gentle; be patient, bearing with one another in love." God has blessed you and Deacon Fred Brown with a son, which makes your life a gift from God.

A Stalwart Woman of God

Deborah Burns

D   Deborah Burns, you are a jewel every step of the way, as you volunteer to

E   employ your help to me, God's way.

B   Because of your love, I must say

O   only God gives you the desire to

R   reach out to others and be a "disciple of Christ." You do it without dismay. Every time you reach out to me, others can see God's love from

A   A to Z so others can see the

H   human side of reaching out is about God's grace.

B   Being a "Disciple of Christ," love is at the center of your life because you

U   understand how to put God's Word into action when you

R   reach out to others with a helping hand.

N   New mercies God gives you every step of the way from
S   sunrise to sunset.

How do I know? I use your legs to point out items on my charts when I teach Sunday school. You also exhibit leadership with the "Lungevity Ministry." This program is designed to help those with lung diseases.

You are a stalwart woman of God. According to Ephesians 2:10 (ESV), "For we are workmanship, created in Christ Jesus for good works, which God prepared beforehand, that we should walk in them."

Records show that you are a Phi Beta Kappa graduate of Howard University and hold a master's degree from Howard's School of Architecture and Planning.

Deborah, you serve mankind in so many ways. God put it in your heart to invest your time in the "Lungevity Ministry" because your husband died of lung disease. God has blessed you with a twenty-nine-year-old son. You are a guiding light in his life.

Thank you for all that you do.

A Stalwart Woman and Man of God
Deacon Joe and Monica Callender

Monica Callender

M   Monica, you and Joe are parents who have dreams and hopes for your boys as they journey in life.

O   On this life journey, God has given you dreams for your boys to

N   Never stop pursuing God and to live according to

I   Isaiah 38:19, which reads,

The living, the living, he shall praise thee, as I do this day: the father to the children shall make known thy truth.

As parents, you named your sons with biblical names.

C   Caleb and Zachary.

In the Bible, Caleb was a faithful man of God. Moses sent out scouts to explore Canaan, one of the twelve men was Caleb. Caleb like Joshua, came back with a glowing report of the riches of the land and with total enthusiasm for going up and taking it. When the people refused to move forward, frightened by the other scout's report of the enemy's strength, Caleb was one of just four men who urged trusting and obeying the Lord. Caleb and Joshua were the only adults of the Exodus generation left alive when the Israelites finally did enter Canaan some forty years later. From the accounts of the life of Caleb, we see a faithful man who trusted God to fulfill his promises when others allowed their fears to override their small faith.

Zachary's name means "The Lord has remembered." The name Zachary is attached to being the father of John the Baptist.

A   As parents, you have hopes and dreams for your boys. You are training and teaching them now in the whole

C   counsel of God so they will know the truth, and nothing but the truth. You are parents with an

A   amazing grace. I believe you teach your sons to

L   live a life with no regrets because

L   life is an adventure and they must live by the power of the Holy Spirit. As parents, you are

E   excellent examples of helping your sons experience life on their terms. You are teaching them to

N   never stop pursuing God. As their parents, you have taught them to

D   dream and for them to

E   explore and live life of no

R   regrets.

Joe and Monica Callender, you are stalwart parents of God who teach and train your sons to serve and love the Lord. Proverbs 22:6 tells us to, "Train up a child in the way he should go: and when he is old, he will not depart from it."

Monica and Joe, what can I say? Just keep on doing it God's way.

Deacon Joe Callender

J   Deacon Joe Callender, God has truly blessed you with the spiritual gift of studying and the teaching of His Word. As a teacher, you have extraordinary and

O   outstanding qualities to

E   explore the Word by searching the scriptures, and treasuring them up in our hearts. You have been entrusted with the task of communicating what the Bible says, what it means, and how we as followers of Jesus Christ are to apply it to our lives here and now. God has also blessed you as an adult Sunday school teacher to

C   cultivate the fruit of the Spirit in our lives with love, joy, peace, longsuffering, gentleness, goodness, faith, meekness, temperance (Gal. 5:22-23).

A   As a teacher, you effectively communicate what the Bible says, what it means and how to

L   live a

L   life-long process, where you keep learning, growing, and depending on God. You pursue

E   excellence in all that you do. The way you teach is aligned with your understanding of God, Jesus Christ, and the Holy Spirit. Your

N   noble character as a teacher, focuses on the Word of God and seeks the spiritual growth of others. You

D   demonstrate in your teaching style that the greatest example of an effective teacher is Jesus Christ. Nicodemus is recorded in scripture as saying to Jesus, "We know that thou art a teacher come from God"(John 3:2). It is

E   evident that you have a strong

R   relationship with God.

Deacon Joe Callender, you graduated from Howard University, Washington, D.C. with a B.S. degree in Mathematics. You also attended the University of Maryland for further study in mathematics.

Deacon Callender, you are a stalwart man of God with the gift to teach and pray in order to build up the body of Christ (Eph. 4:11-12). Paul writes in this scripture that Christ gave some to be apostles, some to be evangelists, some to be prophets, some to be pastors and teachers in order to equip God's people for the works of service so that the body of Christ may be built up. Thank God for your service.

A Stalwart Woman of God

Patricia Anne Chew

P Patricia Anne Chew, your life as a stalwart woman of God consists of your God-given gifts and talents. You excel

A as a flutist and an artist.

T The Word in 1 Timothy 4:14 (NIV) tells us, "Do not neglect your gift, which was given you through prophecy when the body of elders laid their hands on you." In

R response to God's call, you embraced God's desire to use your gift and talent. I believe your response to your gift was like the psalmist,

I "I praise you, for I am fearfully and wonderfully made. Wonderful are your works; my soul knows it very well" (Ps. 139:14 ESV).

C 2 Corinthians 3:3 (NIV) conveys that the Holy Spirit unites His law in our hearts. You have expressed to your family and others,

I "I press on no matter of the struggle." Your gifts and abilities according to 1 Peter 4:10-11 states,

A "As every man hath received the gift, even so minister the same one to another, as good stewards of the manifold grace of God."

C 2 Corinthians 3:3 states, "Forasmuch as ye are manifestly declared to be the epistle of Christ ministered by us, written not with ink, but with the Spirit of the living God; not in tables of stone, but in fleshly tables of the heart." You

H help the body of Christ when you perform as a flutist. God has

E entrusted in you with gifts and abilities. You are a responsible person who lives by and trusts God by managing your gifts. Patricia Anne Chew, your daughter calls you a, "wildflower because you bloom in every season, whatever the terrain."

W We benefit from the talent and gifts God has given you. Sharing your gifts and talent with others can create lasting fulfillment.

Patricia Anne Chew, you are a stalwart woman of God who is faithful to your calling. At the age of ten, you started playing the flute. Music and painting have always been a star in your crown. You attended music camps at Virginia State University, Petersburg, Virginia from 1965-1967. You also took music and writing classes at George Washington University, Washington, D.C. God has truly blessed you in your endeavors.

You are blessed with a daughter, Erica Chew, who is a journalist.

A Stalwart Woman of God

Deaconess Phyllis Davenport

P   People like you with a background as a social worker

H   have hope to follow through to help people in poverty.

Y   Your power switch focuses on reaching out to the needy and educating the public about the needs of poor people. It is

L   like a beautiful rainbow

L   laying in the sky to remind us of the great worldwide flood in the book of Genesis to remove sinful and evil-minded men from the earth.

I   It's God's story of the

S   seven rainbow colors[12] that must pass by:

Red	(Passion/Physical Energy/Aggression/Security)
Orange	(Creativity/Fun & Enjoyment/Exploring)
Yellow	(Happiness/Communication/Clear & Analytical Thinking)
Green	(Health, Nature, Growth, Wealth)
Blue	(Calming/Peaceful/Knowledge/ Communication)
Indigo	(Spiritualism/Mysteriousness/Inward Thinking)
Violet	(Mystery/Imagination & Creativity/ Royalty/Luxury)

When they exist, it is God's glory and power speaking to us to attain spirituality, good health, help to the needy, and wisdom whenever it rains. You are

D devoted

A always giving to others with a

V vision that the needy will succeed and will

E enhance self-awareness to meet their needs. You always tell them to

N never give up but to

P pray to

O our God in order to

R reach their destiny even in the rain because

T the colors of the rainbow are for each of us to obtain.

Deaconess Phyllis Davenport, you are a stalwart woman of God who stands on the Word of Matthew 5:42 (NIV), "Give to the one who asks you, and do not turn away from the one who wants to borrow from you."

Matthew 5:16 (NIV) says, "In the same way, let your light shine before others, that they may see your good deeds and glorify your Father in heaven."

Proverbs 19:17 (NIV) says, "Whoever is kind to the poor lends to the Lord, and he will reward them for what they have done."

Your background indicates that you are a graduate of Lincoln University in Jefferson City, Missouri, and have done graduate work at the University of Maryland, College Park. You have been employed at Milledgeville, State Hospital in Milledgeville, Georgia, and St. Elizabeth's Hospital in Washington, D.C., as a member of the social services staff.

On September 18, 2004, The People's Community Baptist Church, Silver Spring, Maryland, honored you as a charter member of the church and a community leader. Many tributes were made from the office of the president of Lincoln University, and Lincoln University Alumni Association. Douglas M. Duncan, County Executive also sent warm greetings.

You and your husband, Chester, produced a great family. Your son, Corey, and his wife, Siobhan, have given you two grandchildren, Chase, age thirteen, and Carys, age fourteen. God has also blessed you with a devoted daughter, CeCe, and your son-in-law, Robert Berkowitz.

God bless you, Phyllis Davenport, for all that you do to help mankind. God is pleased with your faithfulness.

A Stalwart Man of God

Jonathan Davis

J   Jonathan Davis, Minister of Music of The People's Community Baptist Church, God has given you the gift of conducting music for His glory.

O   Only in relationship with Jesus Christ, our Savior, you are productive.

N   No music can rival the wonder and breathtaking beauty of the Savior, who came as a man to live a perfect life and died

A   an atoning death in our place.

T   The joy your music provides benefits our souls and

H   honors our Savior. One can look back

A   at your past, growing up with a gifted mother of music and a father who also was an encourager. Jonathan, music comes from your soul.

N   Nothing can stop you because you

D   don't let your music be shaped by the influences of the ,
world. Instead, you offer practical help for pursuing
godliness through the grace of the gospel.

A   As a musician, you appreciate a wide variety of different styles and expressions of music. Jonathan, God
has given you a

V   vision to bring glory to Him.

I   1 Peter 2:9 states, "But ye are a chosen generation, a
royal priesthood, an holy nation, a peculiar people;
that ye should shew forth the praises of him who hath
called you out of darkness into his marvellous light."
Your music reflects on Psalms 105:2,

S   "Sing unto him, sing psalms unto him: talk ye of all his
wondrous works."

Jonathan Davis, your music comes from your soul. Your
passion, your heart, put in together, creates your music. When
you perform and minister, we can feel it. Your music calms
our hurried spirits, encourages our troubled hearts, and
strengthens our weary souls. But most of all, like all of God's
gifts; it is meant to draw our hearts and attention to God's
glory, His power, and His love.

God blessed you to attend the University of Maryland
College Park. You received a Bachelor of Arts degree in
Jazz Studies.

You are a stalwart man of God with your music at The
People's Community Baptist Church under the anointed

leadership of Reverend Dr. Haywood Robinson III. You are married to your lovely wife, April. Thank you for your service to the music ministry.

A Stalwart Woman of God

Deaconess Jacqueline Dennard (Jackie)

J   Jacqueline, you are a star in a crown for others to see how you

A   always reach out to help people in need in order for them to succeed.

C   Committed as an advocate and director of a community services foundation, and director of the Health and Social Action Ministry at The People's Community Baptist Church is

K   knowledge that God our Father, and Jesus Christ, our Savior, taught you that life is a place of service you must do each day.

I   In spite of the hardships of others that you witness, God knows your calling, so keep on doing it God's way.

E   Every step you have taken to reduce poverty and to increase self-sufficiency in others is a gift from God because you

D   depend on God's guidance to give you the faith to do your best. Your

E   enthusiasm makes your life a success. You are

N   noble as you work with those you serve and those you work with because

N   nothing separates you from the love of God

A   and your directions come from God above.

R   Reality, according to Jesus, is the establishment and growth of a kingdom on earth of inner loyalty, which transcends all human barriers.

D   Dedication and justice for all is your theme song because you live a life for others.

Deaconess Jacqueline Dennard, you are a stalwart woman of God. God bless you for your service. You demonstrate Proverbs 19:17 (NIV) which says, "Whoever is kind to the poor lends to the Lord, and he will reward them for what they have done." It is the strength that God gives you to be successful in helping others.

God blessed you to receive a Bachelor of Science degree in Social Science from Fort Valley State College, Fort Valley, Georgia, and a master's degree in educational administration and supervision from Howard University in Washington, D.C.

God has blessed you with a son, Francis Dennard of Silver Spring, Maryland. He received a pharmacy degree from Hampton University.

Thank you, Jacqueline, for your service to mankind.

A Stalwart Woman of God

Anne Dyer

A   Adventurous you are, active, always giving to others your love, and

N   nothing stops you because your directions are from above. You speak in the

N   name of Jesus to

E   embrace God's love because in the

D   despair and darkness that you observe in people, God provides

Y   you with directions because He taught you through His Word,

Galatians 6:2, "Bear ye one another's burden and so fulfill the law of Christ." Life is a place of service, and in that service one experiences a great deal of joy.

E   Every other Monday evening under the anointing of
     God, you conduct Bible study in your home or in the
     community. Your life is
R   real because your relationship is intimately bound up
     with your relationship with your fellow man.

Anne Dyer, you are a stalwart woman of God because you
live by faith and God's grace, submitting to God to fulfill your
part in His purpose for you. Without His gift of grace, we
would never have godly faith. God has given you the power
source of life, which is the Word of God. You demonstrate this
in your music, Bible study, and your daily living.

In 1980, you graduated from Hampton Institute, now
Hampton University with a Bachelor of Science degree in
Journalism and Communication. You and your husband,
Minister Milton Dyer, have two wonderful adult daughters,
Merissa and Amber. Thank you for being a servant to mankind.

A Stalwart Man of God

Minister Milton Dyer

M Minister Milton Dyer, God has called you to the ministry, and

I it is an honor to be channeled through God's love because it

L lifts our spirit as a minister of God.

T Through the Word of God, Philippians 3:14 says, "I press toward the mark for the prize of the high calling of God in Christ Jesus."

O Only God can call and grant you the gifts necessary for service. When John

N Newton wrote, "Amazing Grace," he said, "None but He who made the world can make a minister of the gospel." Only God can call a true minister, and only He can grant the minister the gifts for service."

D Down in your heart, there is a melody of praise to serve.

Y   You have the characteristics of an effective minister because you are a faithful steward of God's Word and you rely on God's power.

E   Effective ministers like you are willing to suffer for the chance of the calling.

R   Remember, rely on God's power each and every day as you serve as a faithful servant, and do it God's way.

Minister Dyer, you are a stalwart minister of God. You can't help it. Because your call is authentic, you also sense the gifts necessary for ministry.

God bless you!

The records show that you graduated from Hampton Institute in 1979, now Hampton University, and pursued a B.S. degree in Recreational Administration. In 1985, you received a Master of Business Administration-Finances degree. You are married to Anne Dyer and blessed with two daughters, Merissa, Amber, and a son, Duane King.

God bless you for your service to mankind.

A Stalwart Woman of God

Retired Rear Admiral Evelyn J. Fields

E   Evelyn J. Fields, you are a, "...nail in a sure place..." (Isa. 22:23) with the historical background of being the first African American and first woman to become director of the National Oceanic and Atmospheric Administration (NOAA) Commissioned Officer Corps. Your accomplishments speak

V   very loudly because

E   every step that you took reflected on Joshua 1: 9 (AKJV), "Be strong and of a good courage; be not afraid, neither be thou dismayed: for the Lord thy God is with thee whithersoever thou goest."

Your historical background also lets us know that

L   life is, "But by the grace of God I am what I am: and his grace which was bestowed upon me was not in vain; but I laboured more abundantly than they all: yet not

I, but the grace of God, which was with me" (1 Cor. 15:10 AKJV).

Y   You grew up in a courageous home with stalwart parents who had no limits on what you could do.

N   Nobody but God filled your heart with the aspiration to enlist in the NOAA Corps.

J   James 2:24 (ESV) tells us, "You see that a person is justified by works and not by faith alone."
    However, you kept the

F   faith and you fought the good fight until you finished the race. You are portrayed as an

I   inspirational person. I remembered you as a teenager in my Sunday school class at Second Calvary Baptist Church, Norfolk, Virginia. You were

E   enthusiastic and at that time, were deciding on your career. You requested a recommendation from me when you were in the decision making process about the NOAA Corps. The goal of

L   life is imminent in each thought, word, and leads to fulfillment. The

D   destiny you sought in 1971 began your career with NOAA as a civilian cartographer at the Atlantic Marine Center in Norfolk, Virginia. You were armed with a bachelor's degree in mathematics from Norfolk State College, now Norfolk State University. This destiny led you with the thought to

S   serve mankind.

Evelyn J. Fields, you are truly a stalwart woman of God. According to history, you had a thirty-two-year career with NOAA. You served on many NOAA ships including Mount Mitchell and Peirce, and held the executive officer position on Rainier while researching hydrographic survey vessels. You rose in rank with the Hydrographic Survey Division, serving as chief, and as the administrative officer for the National Geodetic Survey.

In 1995, you became director of the Commissioned Personnel Center in Silver Spring, Maryland. In 1997, you became the Deputy Assistant Administration of the National Ocean Services. In 1989, NOAA selected you as the first woman to command a federal ship. This promotion also marked the first time an African American woman was given the responsibility of commanding a U.S. commissioned ship for any extended duration.

In 1999, President Bill Clinton appointed you as director of the NOAA Corps. You were the first African American to serve as director of NOAA Corps, which came with a simultaneous promotion to Rear Admiral of the NOAA Corps. You were the first woman and first African American to serve as director of the Office of Marine and Aviation Operations and the first to hold the rank of Rear Admiral. You retired in 2003 from NOAA and now live in Florida.

You have received many awards for your service to mankind.

- Received The Bachelor Benedict Club's Lady of the Year Award in Norfolk, Virginia in 1994
- Named by the National Technical Association as one of the top fifty minority women in the science and engineering fields in 1996
- Received the Congressional Black Caucus' Ralph M. Metcalfe Health, Education and Science Award and Woman of the Year from Maryland Federation of Business and Professional Women's Club in 1999
- Received a gold medal from the U. S. Department of Commerce in 2000 for your leadership
- Honored in 2000 by the Virginia Legislature creating a joint memorial resolution for your work in and for the city of Norfolk.

Retired Rear Admiral Evelyn Fields, God blessed you for blessing others. The service that you have rendered to mankind is real service, which cannot be bought or measured with money. Your sincerity and integrity will always be in the history book.

A Stalwart Man of God

Kevin Fisher

K   Kevin Fisher, your knowledge of God's Word is your spiritual gift from God.

E   Evidence is shown when you read and interpret the scripture during our Sunday school sessions. The

V   vastness of God's Word and

I   interest in the knowledge of the Word you seek each Sunday in class.

N   Nothing stops you for

F   finding this knowledge is faith, God's way.

I   In Romans 15:14 (NIV) Paul writes, "that you yourselves are full of goodness, filled with knowledge and competent to instruct one another." The

S   Scripture emphasis in 1 Corinthians 12:8 (NIV) states, "To one there is given through the Spirit a message of wisdom, to another a message of knowledge by means of the same Spirit..." Kevin, your

H   help comes from God. You

E   exercise your gift. In 1 Timothy 4:14, Paul advised Timothy, "Neglect not the gift that is in thee..." because your

R   relationship with God directly impacts your relationship with others.

Your only daughter and child, Nailah Fisher, graduated from St. John University in New York. You encouraged her to seek the gifts God has given her.

Kevin Fisher, you are a stalwart man of God.

A Stalwart Woman of God

Cynthia Givens

C Cynthia Givens, you are a born leader, willing to work in a collaborative effort with the pastor and other musicians.

Y You are an excellent singer who knows the rules and techniques that make a vocal performance stand out. You are a born leader of music with a

N natural instrumentality and the special ability and

T talent to speak to God through music. You also

H have the charismatic gift of grace, which is unmerited favor of God.

I In 1 Peter 4:10, the Word speaks of serving grace. You have been commissioned to ministry, to service. God provides the necessary resources for you to do the work He has given you to do. You make your gift

A a badge of spirituality rather than pride.

G   God is working through your life to do His work in our church and the world.

I   In 1 Corinthians 14:26 it says, "How is it then, brethren? when ye come together, every one of you hath a psalm, hath a doctrine, hath a tongue, hath a revelation, hath an interpretation. Let all things be done unto edifying." The body of Christ is made

V   visible to others. This is the purpose of the body. It is evident that

E   each member of the male chorus functions as one body.

N   Nothing stops you from serving out your giftedness for God's glory when you do it God's way. Your

S   service as director of the men's choir gives great value to the worship service.

Cynthia Givens, you are a stalwart woman of God. You are a super vocalist, which was a gift from God at the age of five years old.

Your records show that you were born in Pittsburg, Pennsylvania when your mother was forty-seven years old. You are a blessing to The People's Community Baptist Church, Silver Spring, Maryland under the pastoral ministry of Reverend Dr. Haywood Robinson, III.

You and your husband, Leonard Givens, have three adult children, Leonard Jr., Eric Anthony, and a daughter Kelsie.

God has also blessed you with two grandchildren, Treylen, and Jett. Thank you, Cynthia, for being a servant to mankind.

A Stalwart Woman of God

Elizabeth Green

E Dr. Elizabeth Green, you have been a star in my crown for over thirty years. Serving as my reading specialist at Suburban Park Elementary School was an honor. You have lived a meaningful

L life helping others. As an

I instructional specialist on the elementary school level, you conducted workshops to promote the intellectual, social, and physical welfare of students, teachers, and parents. Your

Z zeal for

A achievement reflected on our school and the city-wide slogan,

B "Believe, Achieve, Succeed." God also blessed you to teach Bible study classes to the homeless at Union Mission, Norfolk, Virginia. You are the author of

E   *Etiquette of a Pastor's Wife* and a set of Bible stories for children. You also received the

T   Teacher In Education Award (TIE). God has truly blessed you to

H   help others. You have served as a volunteer hospital chaplain by helping individuals and their families with their spiritual needs in times of crisis.

G   God has given you a meaningful life to

R   reach out to help others. You set the

E   example of promoting the meaning of life noted in Ephesians 6:10

E   encouraging kindness, "Finally, my brethren, be strong in the Lord, and in the power of his might."

N   Nehemiah 8:10 (NIV) states, "...Do not grieve, for the joy of the Lord is your strength."

Dr. Elizabeth Green, you are a stalwart woman of God who has devoted your life to helping mankind. God is pleased with your faithfulness. Your late husband, Reverend Dr. Charles Green, was also a stalwart man of God.

In 1998, you received the Doctor of Divinity degree from Norfolk Theological Seminary and Bible College, Norfolk, Virginia.

You have two adult children, Dr. Alesha Ray, and a son, Courtney Ray, in the United States Air Force.

Thank God for your life.

A Stalwart Pastor of God

Dr. Geoffrey V. Guns

G Reverend Dr. Geoffrey V. Guns, God has blessed you for thirty-six years to shepherd Second Calvary Baptist Church in Norfolk, Virginia. You have

E embraced the call to be a thriving pastor.

O Only God has moved you from one degree of grace to another by being a serving pastor who lives out your faith through your work.

Pastor Guns, your relationship with the

F Father gives you grace and power from the Father because you live a life of connectedness with the heavenly Father, and your church is a sanctuary of prayer, grace, and the dwelling of the presence of God.

F For thirty-six years, you have consecrated yourself to God as a pastor.

Titus 1:8 (NIV) tells us,

R "Rather, he must be hospitable, one who loves what is good, who is self-controlled, upright, holy and disciplined."
You have a strong ability to

E empathize to hurting people.

Y You live a life of prayer that leads the people to receive power from God.

V You are a visionary leader, who constantly builds other leaders, to cast the vision, and change the culture and structure of the church, while doing all of this with an eye for missions, evangelism, and growth. Pastor

G Guns, you are able to preach the gospel of the kingdom of God and build leaders.

U Under God's umbrella, you build other leaders through the power of the Spirit. 2 Corinthians 5:18 (NASB) tells us,

N "Now all these things are from God, who reconciled us to Himself through Christ and gave us the ministry of reconciliation." You are a

S servant leader. Christ was a servant leader. Mark 10:45 (NASB) tells us, "...the Son of man did not come to be served, but to serve..."

Reverend Dr. Geoffrey V. Guns, you are a stalwart pastor of God who has listened to God's voice for thirty-six years.

Your records show that your years at Second Calvary Baptist Church are from June 1983 to the present.

When you became pastor of Second Calvary Baptist Church, you lead the congregation to complete the construction of its current sanctuary, educational/fellowship hall, and an administrative office. On May 21, 2015, the congregation completed the purchase of a large tract of land to construct a new parking lot. The land is bordered by Corprew Avenue, Bellmore Avenue, and Ballentine Boulevard.

Under God's directions, a new ministry model was developed which consisted of an Eight Core Ministry, Pastoral Care, Praise and Worship, Congregational Spirituality Services and Helps, Social Justice Ministry, Missions and Evangelism, Nurture and Discipleship.

Records show that in 1972, you earned a B.S. degree in Business Administration. In 1978, you entered the School of Virginia Union University in Richmond, Virginia, and in 1981, you graduated Summa Cum Laude. In 1985, you completed the requirements for the Doctor of Ministry degree from Howard University School of Religion. In July 1985, Virginia Seminary and College bestowed upon you the Honorary Doctor of Humane Letters degree.

Your life contains many facets. You have been an instructor/seminar leader and lecturer in the National Baptist Congress of Christian Education since 1987. You have written numerous articles for the Christian Education Informer, which is published by the Sunday School Publishing Board of the National Baptist

Convention, U.S.A., Inc. These are just a few of your services to mankind. God has also inspired you to publish several books.

Postscript

Records also show that you served as president of the Virginia Baptist State Convention from 1997 to 2001. Many new programs and ministries were developed. You also served as president of the Tidewater Metro Baptist Ministers Conference from 1996-1998.

Pastor Guns, Reverend Wilbert Mills, Sr. and I thank you for appointing us to develop a program to burn the first mortgage on our home church. It only took eleven months to accomplish this goal. Mortgages are mountains, but we had the faith of a mustard seed to move mountains. It took faith to do it. After this accomplishment, you appointed us to develop a stewardship enlistment program with emphasis on becoming a generous giving church by tithing. We moved forward with this effort in 2014, 2015, and 2016.

The weekly giving soared. Why? As our faith increased, our giving increased. Giving to God should be sacrificial.

Let me close by saying, "Have confidence in your leaders and submit to their authority, because they keep watch over you as those who must give an account. Do this so that their work will be a joy, not a burden, for that would be of no benefit to you" (Heb. 13: 17).

You are married to first lady Rosetta Guns. You are blessed with two adult daughters and three grandchildren.

Thank you again for your service to mankind.

A Stalwart Woman of God

First Lady Rosetta Guns

R   Rosetta Guns, as first lady of my home church, Second Calvary Baptist Church, Norfolk, Virginia, memories are locked in my heart and mind about you. When my husband, Reverend Wilbert Mills, Sr. retired in 2011 as pastor of Warren Grove Missionary Baptist Church in Edenton, North Carolina, you became our first lady.

O   On the shoulders of God, each year you preached a Christmas sermon about the blessings and faith in God and how to have a

S   servant's heart. It was

E   evident that your Christian life had a great impact on your career as a social worker. You have helped the homeless, low-income families, addressing their basic needs by helping them get access to food, clothing, and shelter. Romans 12:1 (NIV) expresses your reasonable service,

T "Therefore, I urge you, brothers and sisters, in view of God's mercy to offer your bodies as a living sacrifice, holy and pleasing to God--this is your true and proper worship." "For even the Son of Man did not come to be served, but to serve, and to give His life a ransom for many" (Mark 10:45 NKJV). In

T today's constantly changing and high-stress society, many people get overwhelmed and need assistance and resources to help live better lives. Sister Rosetta Guns, I believe that

A Acts 20:35 (MSG) tells you, "...In everything I've done, I've demonstrated to you how necessary it is to work on behalf of the weak and not to exploit them. You'll not likely go wrong here if you keep remembering that our Master said, 'You're far happier giving than getting.'" According to Hebrews 6:10 (NIV),

G "God is not unjust; he will not forget your work and the love you have shown him as you helped his people and continue to help them."

U Under the umbrella of a social worker, you addressed the basic needs of the low class by helping a family get access to food, connecting homeless persons with shelters, and other resources.

Even after your retirement, you demonstrated in Romans 12:11 (NIV),

N   "Never be lacking in zeal; but keep your spiritual fervor, serving the Lord."

S   Sister Rosetta, I believe that the overall aim of your career as a social worker was to improve the quality of life for your clients.

In today's high-stress society, many people get overwhelmed but you have continued serving in Africa with your husband.

First lady Rosetta Guns, you are a stalwart woman of God who has spent many years helping mankind. Proverbs 19:17 (MSG) describes you as a social worker, "Mercy to the needy is a loan to God, and God pays back those loans in full." May God continue to bless you and our pastor, Reverend Dr. Geoffrey V. Guns.

Your records show that you received your Bachelor of Social Work and Master of Social Work from Norfolk State University, Norfolk, Virginia.

You and Pastor Guns are blessed with two daughters, Nicole Guns Edwards and Kimberly Guns. Kimberly has two children, Kennedy Cummings, age sixteen, and Sydney Cummings, age twelve. Your children's grandfather, Reverend Frank Guns, Sr. is still active in their life.

God bless you as a servant to mankind.

A Stalwart Woman of God

Lydia Harris

L   Lydia Harris, your life as a FedEx employee calls for you to successfully transfer and deliver goods to intended destinations.
For thirty

Y   years, many people have crossed your path daily. Even though you were

D   delivering goods, you were also delivering the Word of God as a *prayer warrior* to persons who crossed your path and who had specific needs.

I   In spite of the fact that your job with FedEx was priority, you

A   aligned your heart, so God would use you as a prayer warrior, as a priority.

H He is your priority. God heard your prayers when you prayed for a cancer patient who became a cancer survivor after your prayer. This person was a negative person who became kind. 1 John 5:14 (NIV) says that God

A always hears. "This is the confidence we have in approaching God: that if we ask anything according to his will, he hears us."

R Romans 8:26-27 (NIV) describes the importance of the Holy Spirit to pray for us, "In the same way, the Spirit helps us in our weakness. We do not know what we ought to pray for, but the Spirit himself intercedes for us through wordless groans. And he who searches our hearts knows the mind of the Spirit, because the Spirit intercedes for God's people in accordance with the will of God."

Philippians 4:6-7 instructs us to pray about everything and present your

R requests to God.

I Isaiah 1:18-19 says, "Come now, and let us reason together, saith the Lord: though your sins be as scarlet, they shall be as white as snow; though they be red like crimson, they shall be as wool. If ye be willing and obedient, ye shall eat the good of the land."

Psalms 5:12 (NIV) states,

S "Surely, Lord, you bless the righteous; you surround them with your favor as with a shield."

Lydia Harris, you are a stalwart woman of God. You motivate and encourage others through your prayers about Christ's love and salvation to assist in strengthening their faith and to push them to their next best level in their walk with God. You are truly a prayer warrior.

God has blessed you and your husband, Richard, Jr., with two daughters, Breanna, age twenty-five, Madison, age thirteen, and a son, Richard III, age twelve. Your background shows that you have a Certificate of Office Technology from Control Data, Pikesville, Maryland. Thank God for your service to mankind.

A Stalwart Woman of God

Yvonne Harris

Y   Yvonne Harris, your life has always been one of standing
     by your child. Luke 6:38 (NIV) is a

V   verse that describes you. It says, "Give, and it will be
     given to you. A good measure, pressed down, shaken
     together, and running over, will be poured into your
     lap. For with the measure you use, it will be measured
     to you." You learned that when one controls his or her

O   own behavior in order to model for his or her child
     how to cope effectively without using physical violence.
     Galatians 6:9 (NIV) tells us as parents, do

N   "...not become weary in doing good, for at the proper
     time we will reap a harvest if we do not give up." When
     your son had problems

N   navigating his life, you did not desert him. God gave
     you insight in all your

E   efforts. Your passion was in restoring

H   hope for your son and connecting him to Jesus through
    your prayers. You prayed to God that your son would
    be free from

A   an addicted gang warfare life. Your son's

R   rest was peaceful because he learned to navigate his life
    by turning to God and he learned to

R   rejoice in a life of self-respect and the glory of God's
    love. Yvonne, your son is not living now, but he was an

I   inspiration to people who have gone astray from the
    way of truth. Galatians 6:9 (NLT) says,

S   "So let's not get tired of doing what is good. At just the
    right time we will reap a harvest of blessing if we don't
    give up." Your son shared his struggles in writing about
    his life behind bars.

Yvonne Harris, you are a stalwart woman of God because
you stood by your son. You also stood on the Word of God
in Matthew 6:33 (NLT), "Seek the Kingdom of God above
all else, and live righteously, and he will give you everything
you need."

Yvonne Harris, you are my first cousin and I can remember
you as a bright young lady who was gifted and talented.

You were the first and only African American to graduate from North Central High School, Indianapolis,
Indiana in 1958.

In 1977, you received an associate degree in business administration from the University of Indianapolis and in 1988, a B.S. degree in General Studies from Indiana University.

You have been married to Frederick Harris for forty-one years. You have one granddaughter, Kiarah Yvonne Harris, daughter of your deceased son, Frederick Walton Harris, Sr. Kiarah is a 2019 high school graduate and has received a four-year scholarship to attend the University of Indianapolis. She also received a scholarship from Gamma Phi Delta Sorority. In 2019, she plans to attend the University of Indianapolis to major in social work. Your grandson, Frederick Walton Harris, Jr. is a certified fork lift truck driver.

Thank you for all you do for mankind.

A Stalwart Man of God

Deacon George T. Hudgens

G   Deacon George T. Hudgens, you stand tall as a stalwart man because of your historic background and your profound career as Colonel in the U.S. Army.

E   Even in the midst of segregation in your hometown, Van Buren, Arkansas, in 1957, you were involved in the initial integration of the school system.

Following graduation from high school, you enrolled at Arkansas Tech University and became the first African American to graduate from that institution.

O   Only God moved you from one degree of grace to another. As a stalwart man, your life in the history books will be

R   remembered because of your faith and your service to mankind. You are a person who persevered to pursue your goals, regardless of the circumstances.

G   God ordered your steps and after twenty-nine years of active duty in the army, you retired from the U.S. Army at the rank of colonel. As a civilian, your second career was Chief Executive Officer and National Director for organizations that provide juvenile justice services. You are an

E   encourager like the words of Joshua 1:9 (NIV), "Have I not commanded you? Be strong and courageous. Do not be afraid; do not be discouraged, for the Lord your God will be with you wherever you go."

T   The records show that your military career was high-lighted by various assignments of increased responsibility. You served as a commander in Vietnam and led the mechanized infantry battalion at Fort Carson in Colorado. In 1983, you became a regimental commander at the U.S. Military Academy, West Point. You were responsible for the supervision, training, development, and welfare of 2,400 prospective Army officers. Colonel

H   Hudgens, records show that you were chief of staff for the U.S. Armed Forces inaugural committee for President H. W. Bush in 1988 and were deputy director for that committee when your fellow Arkansan, Bill Clinton was inaugurated as president in 1992.

U   Under God's umbrella, you are a "...nail in a sure place..." (Isa. 22:23), because Proverbs 16:3 (NIV) says, "Commit to the Lord whatever you do, and he will establish your plans." God guided your life to be strong and not

D   dismayed.

G   God was your refuge and strength, a very present help in trouble (Ps. 46:1). Colonel Hudgens,

E   even today as a member of The People's Community Baptist Church, in Silver Spring, Maryland, you are a stalwart man of God serving as a deacon and a mentor of youth. Your wife, Rosanna, is also an active member of The People's Community Baptist Church.

N   Nothing separates you from the love of God because people who

S   show bravery or courage keep on going, even when things get hard. You are truly a stalwart man of God and you will always be remembered in the history books as the first African American to graduate from Arkansas Tech University.

The African American Chapter of the Arkansas Tech University Alumni Association presented awards to four individuals and one group during the 2018 George T. Hudgens Evening of Excellence at the Lake Point Conference Center in Russellville on Saturday, October 20, 2018.

Retired Colonel Hudgens, you are an example of serving mankind with honor, dignity, and perseverance.

A Stalwart Woman of God

Doris Jones

D   Doris Jones, you have lived a life helping others. During your career as a middle school math teacher, you guided your students to be successful. Even after you retired, you continued to offer help.

     Your number

O   one priority has always been to help students succeed. You

R   reached out to students by setting high expectations and encouraging them to succeed. The motto for Norfolk Public Schools was, "Believe, Achieve, Succeed." Your famous last words were,

I   "I know you can do it."

S   Student's success was your number one priority. Proverbs 22:6 (NIV) states, "Start children off on the way they should go, and even when they are old they will not turn from it." You continued to bring

J joy to others. After your retirement in 1980, you tutored students at your home church, Second Calvary Baptist Church in Norfolk, Virginia.

O Only God gives you the strength to attend social functions, Bible study, sorority meetings, and activities in the community. You do not drive, but your church members, sorority sisters, and your designated cab driver take you when you need them.

N Nobody but God gives you the grace to live an abundant life. It is

E evident that helping others goes hand in hand with a meaningful life. You are a "...nail in a

S sure place..." (Isa. 22:23). You let the world know that age is just a number. You are now ninety-four years old but God's Word is spiritual motivation to your spirit.

Sister Doris Jones, you are a stalwart woman of God because you practice giving and kindness. Today you are helping a young man, whose mother was your house cleaner, but she passed away twenty years ago and you fixed up your garage so her teen-aged son would have a place to stay. You reached out to the least of these.

Records show that you are a graduate of West Virginia State University with a Bachelor of Science degree in Mathematics.

You are an active member of the Iota Omega Chapter of Alpha Kappa Alpha Sorority, Inc., Norfolk, Virginia. Thank God for your service to mankind.

A Stalwart Woman of God

Constance A. Kinder

C   Constance A. Kinder, better known as *Auntie Connie*, you are a star that keeps on shining.

O   On God's shoulders you believe, "...with God all things are possible" (Matt. 19:26 NIV).

N   Nothing stops your mission to provide childcare services. For example this past

S   summer, June through August 2019, provisions were made at

T   the Auntie Connie Creative Corner for children to participate in a comprehensive program of art, music, and dance. This program will be year-round. Also,

A   Auntie Connie's Place provides a developmentally full-day program for young children and an afterschool program K through fifth-grade.

1 John 1:5 (NIV) tells us, "...God is light; in him there is

N no darkness at all." Your

C childcare services are designed like home so you feel like home.

E Each child processes experiences uniquely. They learn through playful and meaningful interactions with materials and people. The concept behind the name

A Auntie Connie lies behind a mission and philosophy based on individual differences and the needs of all children. Constance A.

K Kinder, God has blessed you with a background as an alternative education/in-school intervention coordinator with the Montgomery County Public Schools. Also, during your service with the District of Columbia Public Schools, you served as senior high art teacher and art specialist for the Community Academy Public Charter School. You were successful with each program. You believe the Word of Philippians 4:13 which says,

I "I can do all things through Christ who strengtheneth me." God gave you the courage and initiative to explore

N new ideas to advance your mission and philosophy.

D During your eighteen years of service in Prince George's County, the District of Columbia, and Montgomery School Systems, your service has been honorable. The

E   essence of your life is centered on love, strength, family, and education, but most of all on God's purpose and will. You know how to

R   reach for the rock that is higher than you, because Psalms 61:2 tells us, "...when my heart is overwhelmed: lead me to the rock that is higher than I."

Constance A. Kinder, you are a stalwart woman of God with a vision to help mankind. Your childcare services are built upon excellent service, trust, and confidence in the children and parents.

Records show that you are an alumni of Montclair State University, Upper Montclair, New Jersey, where you earned a Bachelor of Arts in Fine Arts, and Seton Hall University, South Orange, New Jersey, where you earned a Master of Arts in Corporate and Public Communications. Currently, you are a doctoral candidate with Walden University, Minneapolis, Minnesota, pursuing a Doctor of Public Administration.

Records also show that you are a native of Newark, New Jersey, and have been living in the Washington, D.C. area for over twenty years.

You are a member of the National Council of Negro Women, Inc., Potomac Valley Section, a lifetime member of Zeta Phi Beta Sorority, Inc., and an active member of The People's Community Baptist Church under the pastoral ministry of Reverend Dr. Haywood Robinson, III, in Silver Spring, Maryland.

You are the daughter of Ruther M. Kinder and the late Robert L. Kinder. You have one daughter, Brianna Antionette. Constance A. Kinder, God is pleased with your faithfulness.

A Stalwart Woman of God

Ethel Lawhon

E   Ethel Lawhon, everything that you do shows dignity from above, because you are an example of

T   the temple of God

H   honoring God and hearing from Him.

E   Each and every day, you

L   let your life show strength for others to see, as you walk and

L   live a life with strength, honor, and dignity.

A   Always sharing the

W   wisdom that you possess, when you

H   hold on to God's unchanging hand for success.

O   Only God made it possible for you to work at the White House and the State Department in the Office of Protocol under President Bill Clinton's Administration.

This lets us know that when we reach out to God for a helping hand, He is there so we can stand.

N   Nobody but God can move you from one degree of grace to your promise land.

Ethel Lawhon, you are a stalwart woman of God. I believe you were selected to work at the White House and the State Department of Protocol because you are a great communicator and your understanding of the world and its people. You have a certain amount of wisdom that comes from God. You are worthy because you build rapport with others easily.

You live a full life. Your primary goal in all of this is to help people come alive. 1 John 1:4 states, "And these things write we unto you, that your joy may be full."

You are also the church clerk at The People's Community Baptist Church, Silver Spring, Maryland under Reverend Dr. Haywood Robinson, III. Thank God for your faithfulness.

A Stalwart Man of God

Brian Lenair

B   Brian Lenair, you are a gifted saxophonist. The

R   real value of your creativity is God's spiritual gift that's indwelled in your spirit. When you perform, you touch the

I   inside of one's soul, which is the true value of music. You have

A   a special gift for music that is nurtured and developed with the creative force of God.

N   Nothing stops you when you are playing because something inside you makes you stay in touch with the creative force. Your musical

L   life shines because it is based on 2 Chronicles 5:13, "The trumpeters and musicians joined in unison to give praise and thanks to the Lord. Accompanied by trumpets, cymbals and other instruments, the singers raised their voices in praise to the Lord and sang: 'He is good, His love endures forever.'" Your music

E   expresses the truth and touches the soul.

N   Nothing stops you because your music gets inside of the audience and just flows.

A   Along your musical journey, you set the stage for jazz education for youth and events that spotlight music appreciation.

Only God has made you one of the greatest contemporary jazz musicians that can blow with the best of them. God made

I   it possible for you at the age of eight years old to be like your dad who was a jazz saxophonist. You are the

R   real thing because God created you to play your saxophone to hit the inside of people and touch the soul.

When I heard you at the morning worship service on Sunday, April 5, 2019, at The People's Community Baptist Church, Silver Spring, Maryland, under the pastoral ministry of Reverend Dr. Haywood Robinson, III, I was blown away with your pure and God-given talent.

You are a stalwart man of God with a special gift from Him that touches you mentally from the inside. Thank you for your service to mankind.

Postscript

Thank God for your faithfulness in using your gift from God.

A Stalwart Woman of God

Sally Lewis

S   Sally Lewis, God has guided your life for many years to give service to mankind.

A   Along your life journey, you worked for over twenty years for an electronic company, Silent TCP Board. With this company, you became an inspector for Silent TCP Board. Your responsibility as an inspector was to maintain quality standards by approving incoming materials, in-process production, and finished products and record quality results. Your

L   life serving humanity is also serving God. When you left TCP, you devoted your

L   life, serving mankind by creating a cleaning service business and serving as a caregiver.

Y   Your reputation cleaning people's homes is second to none. Your clients love you and want you to live with them. Your

L   life story today is to raise a fallen man and put sunshine into a dark life.

E   Each of your clients receives a touch of your love based upon specific needs; taking a client to church, the doctor, or the grocery store. Presently, you have Bible study sessions with a client who has a vision problem. You are also a caregiver to a client who has special needs. Sally Lewis, God has given you the

W wisdom to serve humanity.

I   In your heart, serving humanity is God's gift to you. Remember, serving God is

S   serving mankind.

Sally Lewis, you are a stalwart woman of God. You have learned to make others secure, comfortable, and happy.

You go beyond yourself to serve others. You put sunshine into a dark life. God bless you.

Stalwart Woman of God

Shirley Little

Shirley Little, thank you for

S   Strength, support, and service, as a school psychologist, rendered to me when I was a psycho-educational specialist.

H   Having you as a team leader

I   induced peace and confidence as we worked together to

R   render service to children who had special needs.

L   Like a bridge over troubled waters, we worked together as a team.

E   Each child was evaluated by a multi-disciplinary team.

Y   Your help as team leader measured each child's Individualized Education Program, or IEP. You made a lasting impact on the

L   lives of students. Matthew 5:16 tells us,

I   "In the same way, let your light shine before others, that they see your good deeds and glorify your Father in heaven." Your

T   time and

T   talent

L   left marks of

E   encouragement for children to grow where they were planted. God has never put anyone in a place too small to grow.

Shirley Little, you are a stalwart woman of God, competent and equipped for every good work. I cherish the many years we worked together.

You have been a role model for many people. For twenty-eight years you were a first lady, two years at First Baptist Church Crestwood in Chesapeake, Virginia, and twenty-six years at the Dome of Canaan Baptist Church, Chesapeake, Virginia where your husband, Reverend Dr. Theodore Little was pastor. At the Dome, you were involved in planning an evangelism exploration program and you were a teacher in the area of Black History and the Youth Ministry.

God also blessed you to initiate a Bible study program at the Tidewater Detention Home in Chesapeake, Virginia. This program has been in operation for thirty-three years.

Under your husband, Reverend Dr. Theodore Little's administration, Dome of Canaan was a tithing church, one hundred percent. Every member was a tither.

God blessed you to receive a Bachelor of Science degree in Sociology from Livingston College, Salisbury, North, Carolina, and a Master of Arts degree in Education Psychology from Atlantic University, now Clark Atlanta, Georgia. Shirley Little, thank you for your service to mankind.

1 Thessalonians 5:11 (NASB) tells us, "Therefore encourage one another and build up one another, just as you also are doing."

You and your husband are blessed with two adult daughters, Reverend Lisa Little of Chesapeake, Virginia, and Kellie Little of Stafford, Virginia.

Thank you for your service to mankind.

A Stalwart Man of God

Deacon James H. Lockhart

J   Deacon James Lockhart, God has blessed you to wear many hats each and every day.

A   Along this life journey, He wants you to tell the world about His gift to you, as you tarry His way. As a deacon you,

M   meet the spiritual needs of the members of the church when you write and publish books about faith, love, and fun. You express your ideas so the readers can get a picture of your thoughts and insight.

E   Even when things look blight, you find insight, because the

S   Scripture says, "I can do all things through him who gives me strength" (Phil. 4:13 NIV). Brother Lockhart, you

H   have a heart given by God to inspire others. Psalms 45:1 (NIV) says, "My heart is stirred by a noble theme as I recite my verses for the king; my tongue is the pen of a skillful writer." In your heart

L   life will, "Never be lacking in zeal, but keep your spiritual fervor, serving the Lord" (Rom. 12:11 NIV). You have shown that you have the

O   obligation and creativity to represent God as a writer. Your

C   call to write as a faithful steward of God's grace

K   keeps our

H   hearts

A   alert,

R   righteous, and

T   thankful for the Word of God.

Deacon Lockhart, you are a stalwart man of God. According to Jeremiah 1:4-10, you have found God's plan for your life. Thank you for sharing your thoughts through your writings. God has blessed you as a published author, playwright, and poet. You are also an honor graduate of LaSalle (Military) Institute, Troy, New York; Scholarship (B.A.) and Fellowship (M.A.) graduate of the State University of New York Albany; Education Doctorate (Ed.D.) Columbia University Teachers College, New York; as well as high level, professional services with New York State Department of Education; The State

University of New York at Albany History Department; Ford Foundation's Washington Internship in Education, as well as thirty-seven years as Senior Educational Program Official, U.S. Department of Education, Washington, D.C. God blessed you to retire in September 2012.

Deacon Lockhart is married to Maria Carrington Lockhart, Ph.D. Maria is currently a Senior Education Program Specialist with the

U. S. Department of Education in Washington, D.C.

The Lockharts are blessed with a family of loving children: Lawrence Rubama, Michelle Rubama (children of Maria); Jordan and Robert Rubama (grandchildren of Maria). Then there is Angela Lockhart Fisher, Lisa Lockhart McCoy, and Dirk Gavin McCoy.

Deacon Lockhart serves diligently as a deacon and is on the newsletter team at The People's Community Baptist Church, Silver Spring, Maryland under the anointed pastoral ministry of Reverend Dr. Haywood Robinson, III.

A Stalwart Woman of God

Cynthia Marshall-McFarland

C   Cynthia Marshall-McFarland, God has truly blessed you with the gift of music, which is the fairest and most glorious gift of God.

Y   You direct with the main purpose to worship God. Music is

N   next to the Word of God. Your music removes the fascination of evil

T   thoughts and it feeds the soul and

H   holds up the banner of God.
James 5:13 says,

I   "Is any among you afflicted? let him pray. Is any merry? let him sing psalms."

A   According to Psalms 95:1, "O come, let us sing unto the Lord: let us make a joyful noise to the rock of our salvation." Cynthia, your

M music talks to us, and pulls at our hearts in unusual ways.

A And it helps develop and lead the worship with the pastor. Your music stores up the ingredients to

R reach feelings and emotions among the congregation, God's way. Your

S songs of hymns amplify ecstatic feelings that we are delighted to be alive. God has blessed you with the ability to select the right piece of music at the right time.

H Hebrews 2:12 tells us, "Saying, I will declare thy name unto my brethren, in the midst of the church will I sing praise unto thee."

A A song of praise is found in Psalms 100:1-2, "Make a joyful noise unto the Lord, all ye lands. Serve the Lord with gladness: come before His presence with singing." Colossians 3:16 states,

L "Let the word of Christ dwell in you richly in all wisdom; teaching and admonishing one another in psalms and hymns and spiritual songs, singing with grace in your hearts to the Lord."
Psalms 95:1 states "O come,

L let us sing unto the Lord: let us make a joyful noise to the rock of our salvation." The

M music that you select are songs of praise that strengthen our capacities for forgiveness, love, and appreciation.

C Cynthia, your music is a "...nail in a sure place..." (Isa. 22:23). It is

F   full of life that moves us from one degree of grace to another. Romans 15:9 tells us,

A   "And that the Gentiles might glorify God for his mercy; as it is
written, For this cause I will confess to thee among the Gentiles, and sing unto thy name." We thank God for you as our music director for finding the

R   right piece of music that worships God in spirit and in truth. What would life be like without it? It is evident that your

L   leadership is demonstrated when you run rehearsals, and create an atmosphere where members can interact freely with God. Cynthia Marshall-McFarland, you are

A   an example of preparation in your role as a music director. Thank God for providing you with

N   new mercies as a

D   devoted music director at The People's Community Baptist Church under the anointed leadership of Reverend Dr. Haywood Robinson, III.

You are truly a stalwart woman of God with the wisdom to direct the Women's Ministry with dignity and love.

Your background indicates that you graduated from Howard University, Washington, D.C.

You are married to a devoted husband, Damon McFarland.

A Stalwart Woman of God

Minister Joan McCarley

J   Joan, you are a minister of God who has demonstrated
    God's call for you to serve Him, Jesus Christ and

O   others as a steward of God.

A   According to 1 Peter 4:10, "As every man hath received
    the gift, even so minister the same one to another, as
    good stewards of the manifold grace of God."

N   Nothing separates you from the love of God to serve as a

M   minister of God because you are equipped by the Holy
    Spirit. Your

C   calling is preaching and teaching the Word of God
    with a growing

C   compulsion. Your call is also

A   authentic and

R   reverent.

L   Like Jeremiah, you have a burning desire to teach and
    preach the Word of God. You
E   exhibit leadership and help to others.
Y   You are wise, having the power of discernment and
    judging properly as to what is true or right.

Minister Joan McCarley, you are a stalwart woman of God
from A to Z. You have accomplished high theological degrees,
but most of all, you know who God is and what He wants you
to do. To God be the glory! You are a Licensed Independent
Clinical Social Worker with a master's degree in social work
from the State University of New York at Buffalo's School of
Social Work. You received a Master of Divinity degree, Summa
Cum Laude, from the Howard University School of Divinity.
In May 2000, you were ordained as a Baptist minister through
the American Baptist Convention. Presently, you serve as an
Associate Minister at The People's Community Baptist Church,
Silver Spring, Maryland under the anointed pastoral ministry
of Reverend Dr. Haywood Robinson, III.

Records show that you have served as a consultant to
national and international organizations and health ministries that include but are not limited to: Thailand, Uganda,
the Netherlands, the United Kingdom, France, Switzerland,
India, Bahamas, etc.

Records also show that you are Executive Director of
TERRIFIC, Inc., a nonprofit organization that provides
housing and human services to families in crisis.

Debbie Tate is president. You and Debbie are co-founders of Grandma's House, a residential care home for children with HIV/AIDS.

God has blessed you to receive many awards and honors for your commitment to humanity, such as: National Coalition of 100 Black Women; International Salute to Martin Luther King Jr. Award. God has also blessed you to be featured in the New York Times, Boston Globe, and many others for your service to mankind.

Minister Joan McCarley, you are a devoted and loving mother of three wonderful, married children and six beautiful grandchildren. God has blessed you to be a dedicated ordained minister and a non-profit executive who has committed your life to seeking to improve the quality of life of marginalized people. God is pleased with your faithfulness.

I thank God for you and your service to mankind.

A Stalwart Woman of God

Gladys McElmore

G   God has truly given you the gift to write about His Word.

L   Like Paul of the Bible, he wrote for the churches and he wrote for the souls.

A   As a freelance writer on religion, you are read each week in the New Norfolk Journal and Guide Newspaper. Your weekly articles are well written and can change a life.

D   Down in your soul, your articles are written so that one will put their faith in Jesus. Acts 20:18 (NKJV) tells us before Paul wrote about Christ, he lived Christ. He responded to a real world with real words. Gladys, you do the same because

Y   you feed hungry people with God's Word by conducting monthly Bible studies for the community and invited people. Gladys, you are the right

S   stuff when you write and plan for the soul and as you

M   move readers to

C   clearly understand God's words because

E   each and every day you seek God's way as you live with integrity.

L   Like Paul, John, and Luke in

M   many of your articles you respond to a real world with real words from the Bible.

O   One can observe from your writing that you write what God

R   reveals to you, and

E   everything that you write is the Word from the Bible.

Gladys McElmore, you are a stalwart woman of God. You are the author of *Embracing Jesus Christ*. This book stresses that faith in Christ is not just assenting to what God is for us, but also embracing all that He is for us in Christ.

This *embracing* is one kind of love for Christ, the kind that treasures Him above all things. Believing that Jesus is the Son of God means *embracing* the significance of that truth. God bless you in your career as a religious writer.

Postscript

You are blessed with a devoted son, James Herman McElmore.

A Stalwart Pastor of God

Reverend Dr. La Verne Wilson-McLaughlin

L   La Verne, it is an honor to call you Reverend because you are an effective and spiritual minister of God.

A   Always willing to carry out God's calling to serve with a

V   vision to bring forth fruit and that fruit, according to John 15:16, God has given you the desire to preach and to be a pastor. God has also

E   equipped you with the gifts necessary for ministry because you are

R   resilient, knowing when to spring back when things fall low. Like Michelle Obama's famous phrase, "When they go low, we go high," your motto is,

N   "Never give up," because you are an

E   example and an effective minister always willing to suffer for the church. You have

M   mentored men and women who were interested in the
    gospel and you encouraged them with a passion. As a
    successful pastor, your mentoring helped others pre-
    pare for the ministry. You also have a
C   compulsion to serve Jesus Christ and the
L   leadership to inspire others as well to have
A   a personal relationship with Jesus Christ. You are
U   undaunted, not discouraged when dealing with prob-
    lems or helping others in need. You are always there to
    lend a helping hand. You are
G   gentle. According to Titus 1:7, "For a bishop must be
    blameless, as the steward of God; not selfwilled, not
    soon angry, not given to wine, no striker, not given to
    filthy lucre," You are
H   hospitable. Titus 1:8 says, "But a lover of hospitality, a
    lover of good men, sober, just, holy, temperate,"
    Your
L   leadership inspires others because you are
I   involved with others to pursue spiritual discipline
    and to help them seek to grow in their relationship
    with Christ.
N   Nothing separates you from the love of God. You focus
    on the needs of people to know the gospel.

Reverend McLaughlin, you are a stalwart woman of God
with a purpose-driven heart to see the church faithfully pursue
God's purposes.

Your background shows that your undergraduate studies started at Capital Bible Seminary in Lanham, Maryland. You obtained your master's degree from Virginia Union University in Richmond, Virginia, and your doctorate from Wesley Theological Seminary in Washington, D.C.

You are married to Reverend Dr. Thomas McLaughlin. Between the two of you, God has blessed you with six children, eight grandchildren, and three great-grandchildren.

God bless you for your service to mankind.

A Stalwart Woman of God

Alean Miller

A   Alean Miller, God has blessed you to work at the National Center for Education Statistics (NCES) for over twenty years. Working in such a

L   learning environment

E   enables you to focus on the role of NCES in education policymaking. According to your profile, you work with contractors and hire researchers. As a former teacher, a guidance counselor and being a child of God, you were glad that NCES in education policymaking was focusing on the

A   achievement of students with special disabilities.

N   NCES has a clear vision for the future. The

M   management is part of the federal government. It lives within the United States Department of Education, which is headed by the Secretary of Education, a member of the president's council. NCES

I   is also part of the Office of Educational Research and Improvement.

L   Longitudinal studies are services provided to support Parent Involvement, Curriculum Designed, and Instructional Practice.

L   Living a life for others is a gift from God.
Colossians 3:23 tells us, "Whatever you do, work at it with all your heart, as working for the Lord, not for human masters," This

E   encourages you to do the best you can every day. As you move forward on your job,

R   remember that your job is connected with spotlighting the condition with the mission of NCES when you hire researchers.

Alean Miller, you are a stalwart woman of God with a mission to assist state and local education agencies in approving their statistical system.

Your background in education has prepared you for the mission to help others.

In 1973, you received an A.A. degree in Journalism from Chipola Junior College in Mariana, Florida; B.A. degree in Special Education from University of South Florida, Tampa, Florida in 1975; Master of Education in Guidance and Counseling from Florida A&M University, Tallahassee, Florida in 1977.

Thank God for your service to mankind.

A Stalwart Man of God

Deacon Timothy Mitchell

T   Deacon Timothy Mitchell, an ordained Deacon and teacher of the Old Testament. God has directed your life to teach His Word. Deacon Mitchell, your teaching

I   is one of the gifts of the Holy Spirit that you possess. We came into the world ignorant and we

M   must be taught sound doctrine based on the written Word of God. The

O   Old Testament text writings are linked to the story of God for all mankind, and especially applicable to the New Testament interpretations. Matthew 28:19 emphasizes

T   teaching, like preaching. It was an integral part of the walk of an apostle. "Go ye therefore, and teach all nations, baptizing them in the name of the Father, and of the Son, and the Holy Ghost." The records show that God

H   has anointed you to teach Sunday school and Bible study classes on the Old Testament.

Y   You press forward with steadfastness in Christ, having a perfect brightness of hope, and a love of God in you.

You teach from the Old Testament in a way that makes students find happiness or when they face unknown trials. Deacon Mitchell, throughout your life you were not only a friend but a teacher. Also, a

M   mentor working with young boys as a scout leader and training parents about parenting. When you traveled

I   internationally, you spread the gospel to hurting people.

T   2 Timothy 2:24 states, "And the servant of the Lord must not strive; but be gentle unto all men, apt to teach, patient..." You demonstrate this as a Sunday school teacher. You are well *qualified* and *reliable*. As a

C   Christian, you have studied and taught from the Old Testament so your classes can find peace which the gospel brings and hope of eternal life. It is evident that the

H   Holy Spirit tells you what to do. You are an

E   encourager to

L   live the absolute and unchanging truth of God. The day is coming when teaching will be unnecessary. "No

L   longer will they teach their neighbor or say to one
     another, 'Know the Lord,' because they will all know
     me, from the least of them to the greatest" (Heb.
     8:11 NIV).
     Jeremiah 31:34 says, "And they shall teach no more
     every man his neighbour, and every man his brother,
     saying, Know the Lord: for they shall all know me,
     from the least of them unto the greatest of them, saith
     the Lord: for I will forgive their iniquity, and I will
     remember their sin no more."

Deacon Timothy Mitchell, you are a stalwart man of
God who has pursued an outstanding background in religion and business. In 1979, at Carnegie Mellon University
in Pennsylvania, you received the Master of Science degree
in Management and Policy Analysis. In 1977, you received a
Bachelor of Arts degree from Carleton College in Minnesota
in Urban Studies. In 1972, at Long Beach City College in
California, you received an associate degree in economics. You
also served as executive vice president of the National Archives
Publishing Company in Michigan.

You and your lovely wife, Panthea, are blessed with three
children. Two are adults, ages forty and thirty-seven, and one
daughter, age seventeen.

Deacon Timothy Mitchell, God has blessed you with a
marvelous life serving mankind.

A Stalwart Woman of God

Dr. Olivia Newby

O   Olivia, you are a woman of valor who

L   lives a life in obedience to the Lord and His people.

I   In today's world, you wear many hats with

V   vigor each and every day, directed by the Holy Spirit. Your

I   inner spirit allows you to rise when you are exhausted, lonely, or trembling.

A   As a stalwart force in the twenty-first century, you help the needy, teach the Word of God as a Sunday school teacher, provide information about life as a conference presenter, and work as a nurse practitioner for your husband, Dr. James Newby, Sr.

N   Nothing stops you because you are a woman of prayer, and you grow in God's grace. God

E   exhorts you to do everything well.

W   What a blessing you are as you help others to excel. Therefore, continue to

B   be brave and stand, because God is at the helm each and every day.

Y   Your life is excellent from A to Z because you do it God's way.

Dr. Olivia Newby, you are a stalwart woman of God. You and your husband have a vegetable garden to feed the hungry as well as conducting workshops to help with other needs. Your concern for the *least of these* is described in Matthew 25:40, "And the King shall answer and say unto them, 'Verily I say unto you, Inasmuch as ye have done it unto one of the least of these my brethren, ye have done it unto me.'"

God is pleased with your faithfulness.

Postscript

I shall always remember Dr. Olivia Newby as a stalwart Sunday school teacher of God. In 1999, when my husband and I returned to our home church, Second Calvary Baptist Church in Norfolk, Virginia under the pastoral ministry of Reverend Dr. Geoffrey Guns, I became a member of Dr. Olivia Newby's Sunday school class. Dr. Newby is a great Sunday school teacher because she is willing to be and willing to do what it takes to make a difference in her students' life despite the many professional backgrounds of her students. She has a deeply sincere, committed heart for God when she teaches.

She exhibits Proverbs 9: 9 (NIV), "Instruct the wise and they will be wiser still; teach the righteous and they will add to their learning."

She also exhibits Romans 12:6-7 (NIV), "We have different gifts, according to the grace given to each of us. If your gift is prophesying, then prophesy in accordance with your faith; if it is serving, then serve; if it is teaching, then teach..."

Dr. Olivia Newby is a family nurse practitioner at Primary Care Specialist in Norfolk, Virginia. She is the co-founder and president of The Healthy Living Center Foundation, a 501(c)(3) nonprofit. Dr. Newby serves as adjunct faculty in the Nursing Graduate College at Old Dominion University in Norfolk Virginia. She holds a bachelor's degree in nursing from Howard University in Washington, D.C., a master's degree in nursing from Hampton University in Hampton, Virginia, a Doctor of Nursing Practice from Old Dominion University, a National Certificate of Diabetes Education, and certification as a Diabetes Lifestyle Coach. Dr. Newby has experience in primary care, entrepreneurship, culinary medicine, research, and diabetes education. She is the vice president/president-elect of Virginia Council of Nurse Practitioners. Dr. Newby was a 2020 inductee of Fellows American Association of Nurse Practitioners and recipient of the 2020 President's Award from Virginia Council of Nurse Practitioners. She is a member of the American Association of Nurse Practitioners, the Virginia Council of Nurse Practitioners, the America Nurses Association, and the Association of Diabetes Care & Education Specialists. Lastly, Dr. Newby is a board member of the American Heart Association Hampton Roads. Dr. Newby possesses professional interests in diabetes and dietary health prevention for at risk populations.

Thank you, Dr. Olivia Newby, for your service to mankind.

You are still my Sunday school teacher because you have a heart for God and a love for people.

Olivia Newby, Ph.D., God has blessed you with a great family. Your husband, Dr. James Newby, is a medical doctor. Your son, James E. Newby, III, J.D., is a computer software engineer. Your daughter, Marcia Newby Goodman, M.D., and her husband have given you two grandchildren.

God has bound your family together with love.

A Stalwart Woman of God

Claudette Overton

C   Claudette Overton, on your life journey, you spent thirty-eight years working as Director of the Norfolk, Virginia Juvenile Court Services Unit. Your

L   life mission was to protect the public through a balanced approach of comprehensive services that prevented and reduced juvenile delinquency through a partnership with families, schools, and law enforcement agencies in order for delinquent youth to develop into responsible and productive citizens. God's

A   amazing grace leads you to

U   understand the youth in your care. You

D   developed youth and family programs that were recognized by the State of Virginia. You were

E   encouraged by Proverbs 3:5-6 (NASB) to,

T   "Trust in the Lord with all your heart and do not lean on your own understanding. In all your ways, acknowledge Him, and He will make your paths straight." Your mountain

T   top experience gave you more courage to lean on the Word of God. James 1: 2-4 (NIV) states, "Consider it pure joy, my brothers and sisters, whenever you face trials of many kinds, because you know that the testing of your faith produces perseverance. Let perseverance finish its work so that you may be mature and complete, not lacking anything." You are an

E   encourager. Proverbs 31: 8-9 (ESV) describes your commitment.

O   "Open your mouth for the mute, for the rights of all who are destitute. Open your mouth, judge righteously, defend the rights of the poor and needy." Norfolk,

V   Virginia holds you in high esteem because before you retired, you were an

E   *encourager,* a

R   *restorer* and a

T   *teacher* to the youth and families in order for them to develop and enhance competencies necessary to sustain healthy and productive lifestyles.

O   Only God allowed you to rise and be successful for thirty-eight years as director of the Norfolk Juvenile Court Services Unit. God gave you

N   new mercies each and every day.

Claudette Overton, you are truly a stalwart woman of God. God is pleased with your faithfulness as you reach out to those who need help.

You have been an active member of Second Calvary Baptist Church, Norfolk, Virginia over thirty years where you serve as a trustee. As a breast cancer survivor, you serve as vice president of the Ministry of Spiritual Support for Cancer. God has blessed you to successfully secure cancer grant funding to support education and awareness for congregants and the community. Currently, you serve as a volunteer with the American Cancer Society. You are a strong believer in God. Your testimony is in Matthew 6:33, "But seek ye first the kingdom of God, and his righteousness; and all these things shall be added unto you."

You have testified that your lifelong philosophy is, "Making a difference in your life by making a difference in the lives of others."

Your record shows that you are a graduate of Norfolk State University with a Bachelor of Science in Business Administration and a master's degree in urban studies (Human Resource Administration).

Claudette Overton, thank God for your service to mankind.

A Stalwart Woman of God

Melisa D. Rawles

M   Melisa Rawles, you are a dynamic youth choir director of The People's Community Baptist Church under the pastoral ministry of Reverend Dr. Haywood Robinson, III, Silver Spring, Maryland.

E   Every fourth Sunday, the abilities of the youth of the church are cultivated to the highest of their potential as a choir. Your strong

L   leadership inspires and motivates the youth choir singers to sing to the glory of God. You have a deep

I   interest and understanding of how music and harmony work. Ephesians 5:19 (NIV) tells us,

S   "speaking to one another with psalms, hymns, and songs from the Spirit. Sing and make music from your heart to the Lord."

Psalms 98:4-5 (NIV) tells us to, "Shout for joy to the Lord...with the harp and the sound of singing..." You are

A   able to establish clear boundaries and positively maintain high expectations with the youth. Because of your success, it is evident that you

R   respond to the concerns of youth and their parents in a sensitive manner.

A   All that you do are praises to God. Your

W   wide range of church music reflects on Colossians 3:16 (NIV), "Let the message of Christ dwell among you richly as you teach and admonish one another with all wisdom through psalms, hymns, and songs from the Spirit, singing to God with gratitude in your hearts." Because of your strong

L   leadership as director of the youth choir, you know techniques that make a vocal performance stand out. Your music program serves the

E   evolving

S   spiritual needs of your youth choir.

Melisa D. Rawles, you are a stalwart woman of God. You have built a youth choir that has been taught the proper mechanics of singing. Their expectations are high about how music and harmony work.

You have a strong sense of musicality. May God continue to bless you for your service to mankind.

Records show that you graduated from the University of Pittsburgh, Pennsylvania with a Bachelor of Science degree in Psychology.

You also graduated from the Catholic University of America, Columbus School of Law. With a lawyer's background, you now work as director of employee relations.

You and your husband, John Woodson, have a daughter, Myla, age ten and a son, David, age twenty-eight.

God bless you for all that you do.

A Stalwart Man of God

Deacon Dewey Reeves

D   Deacon Dewey Reeves, God has blessed you to wear many hats in your life. You retired as principal of Eastern Senior High School in Washington, D.C. In your school,

E   every day was a day of learning. You left your footprints in the sand of time by building an environment of high expectations, a great school climate, and being a great instructional leader.

Presently, you serve as deacon at The People's Community Baptist Church in Silver Spring, Maryland, and a leader of the Men's Rites of Passage, a great program that focuses on developing *boyhood to manhood*.

W   What God has for you is for you. God has given you

E   endurance according to Romans 5:3-4, "And not only so, but we glory in tribulations also: knowing that tribulation worketh patience; And patience, experience; and experience hope."

Y You demonstrate this because you give God your best. It is evident that you have pursued godly character because you

R respond to situations by faith. God has given you the gracious fruit of faith to persevere and to

E endure when you are involved in His Word as stated in

E Ephesians 6:11, "Put on the whole armor of God, that ye may be able to stand against the wiles of the devil." Your

V vision is controlled by God and you seek His presence to do

E everything His way because God's

S sovereignty rules and God is in control of all things and rules over all things.

Deacon Reeves, you are a stalwart man of God in your home, church, and the community. The records show that you are a native of Jackson, Mississippi, and a graduate of Jackson State University with a Bachelor of Arts degree. God blessed you as an educator and administrator for more than thirty-one years. Your life experiences in education and life, in general, moved you from one degree of grace to another. You also received a Master of Science degree in Education Administration and Supervision from Cleveland

State University, Honors: Summa Cum Laude and additional doctoral studies at Kent State University and George Washington University and five consecutive years in the prestigious I/D/E/A Fellows Program at Harvey Mudd College, Claremont, California. You also hold certifications in teaching, administration, and supervision in the District of Columbia, Ohio, and Virginia.

When you were the principal of Eastern Senior High School, Washington, D.C., you developed and installed the Law and Legal Service Academy. This effort was to move the school toward a nationally competitive level. This was accomplished by establishing strong academic guidelines, high expectations, and strong disciplinary guidelines for students, faculty, and staff. Parents were required to be involved from the beginning to the end of the school year. This was established in a Memorandum of Understanding (MOU) with the Honorable Robert Rubin, Secretary of the United States Treasury Department.

After thirteen months of meeting, planning, and negotiating with the Treasury Department, the Law and Legal Service Academy at Eastern Senior High School was born out of this partnership. On October 27, 1999, an official signing of the Memorandum of Understanding was held with the Secretary of the Treasury, Robert Rubin, the academy coordinator and you, as principal. God has also given you the gift in the music realm. You spent a great part of your life in Cleveland, Ohio where you were awarded a Rockefeller Foundation Grant to study the French horn at the Cleveland Institute of Music with Myron Bloom, former principal hornist with the Cleveland Symphony Orchestra. After intensive study, you became a principal hornist in the Beechwood Symphony Orchestra where you performed for thirteen years.

Thank God for your service to mankind.

Deacon Reeves is married to Reverend Sonya Neal Reeves. The Reeves have two children, Malcolm DeAngelo and an adopted daughter, Nicole Brice.

A Stalwart Woman of God

Minister Sonya Reeves

S   Sonya Reeves, God has truly blessed you as a minister of the gospel.

O   On the day of Pentecost, the Holy Spirit filled both men and women alike without concern of gender (Acts 2:1-21).

Minister Reeves, your faithful service is demonstrated in your prayers and any of the vast array of ministry. When you minister, God gives you

N   new mercies to exhibit

Y   your joy, heart and soul

A   along with the Holy Spirit to direct your path.

R   Recorded in 1 Timothy 2:11-15, Paul's advice to Timothy was to not permit, "a woman to teach or to have authority over a man." In Romans 16:1-2, Paul changed to be an advocate of women in the ministry. Reverend Reeves, it is

E   evident that God continues to call women like you to serve alongside men in the vital work of ministry today. You are an

E   example of being qualified to teach and lead within any of the vast array of ministry roles and positions with a biblically qualifying lifestyle. It is

V   vital that women like you continue to move forward in the ministry of The People's Community Baptist Church. It is

E   evident that God wants you to walk in

S   step with the Holy Spirit in power and service.

Minister Sonya Neal Reeves, you are a stalwart woman of God with wisdom and knowledge of the Word of God. Your background shows that you are a senior program analyst with the Planning Resources Conservation Service, U.S. Department of Agriculture. Congratulations on your recent enrollment into the Doctor of Ministry program at the Howard University School of Divinity with a focus of study, Pastoral Leadership and Congregational Formation. You and Deacon Reeves are parents of two children, Malcolm DeAngelo and an adopted daughter, Nicole Brice. Thank God for your service to mankind.

A Stalwart Woman of God

Shirley Ricks

S   Shirley, you served as a parent resource technician for many years to

H   help parents develop skills

I   in parenting and

R   raising their children to be successful in school and to

L   live in deeds and thoughts to succeed in life. As you looked to God for help, your parents

E   endured and found happiness from workshops and conferences that you conducted.

Y   Your blessings did flow with

R   reverence,

I   ideas,

C   commitment and

K   knowledge to pursue

S   success.

Shirley Ricks, you are a stalwart woman of God. You helped parents to become actively involved in their children's education. You stressed an open door policy to encourage parents to want to be involved in their children's education.

You knew your school, your students, your parents, and your community. You encouraged the belief that it is not parent participation alone that is responsible for students reaching their full potential. It is the student's belief in themselves and their ability that make dreams come true. You encouraged that belief and together with your parents and students, you worked on their goals with a dream to fulfill.

Shirley Ricks, you are my sister-in-law, and your principal would share with me how you blessed her school as a parent technician. I believe that you demonstrated Proverbs 22:6, "Train up a child in the way he should go: and when he is old, he will not depart from it."

You attended Norfolk State University and majored in elementary education. You are blessed with a son, McKinley and his wife, Tanisha. You have two granddaughters, Amaya, age twelve, and Avery, age five.

Thank you for your service to mankind.

A Stalwart Man of God

Deacon Anthony E. Rodgers

A   Deacon Anthony E. Rodgers, God has blessed you to serve The People's Community Baptist Church as a devout deacon.

You have a background, which shows that you have served others in many facets of your life. God prepared you to graduate from the University of Maryland with a degree in public health. This background opened doors to live a life for others. You also help develop the Faith Art Academy, which is still in existence. You retired as an Associate Director of the Food and Drug Administration.

N   Nothing separates you from carrying out your duties as a deacon because of your high standing and great confidence in the faith that is in Jesus Christ. According to

T   Titus 2:6-8, "Young men likewise exhort to be sober minded. In all things shewing thyself a pattern of good works: in doctrine shewing uncorruptness, gravity, sincerity, sound speech, that cannot be condemned; that he that is of the contrary part may be ashamed, having no evil thing to say of you."

H   "Holding the mystery of faith..." (1 Tim. 3:9), you demonstrate this because

O   only God gives you the grace to move mountains.

N   Nothing separates you from the love of God.

Y   You are an

E   example of good deeds beyond

R   reproach.

O   Only God gives you the character as a dreamer to move the church forward. As a deacon, God gave you the faith and vision to organize a team to initiate a plan to eliminate the church mortgage. You pursue

D   devoted and

G   godly character by your

E   eagerness and diligence in going after something and completing tasks. Proverbs 24:16 (NET Bible) says, "Although a righteous person may fall seven times, he gets up again, but the wicked will be brought down by calamity." You show

R   reverence for God, desiring to honor, please, and reflect God in everything. God's

S   sovereignty is the most comforting doctrine in all Scripture. Nothing happens in the universe apart from God's sovereign power.

Deacon Anthony E. Rodgers, you are a stalwart man of God. Your godly vision to burn the church mortgage was the understanding of God's Word. A godly vision brings one closer to God. Proverbs 29:18 says, "Where there is no vision, the people perish…" This means that without godly vision, the people will run wild without restraint. You stepped out in faith to pursue the vision that God will meet our needs to burn the mortgage. Vision and leadership are essential in a church and ministry. This vision is truly helping our church move toward a better future.

Deacon Rodgers, you and your wife Sharon, are blessed with four children, Shonta, Shonda, Joie, and Anthony M. Rodgers. Shonda has two children, Alexis and Derrick Jr. Derrick Jr. is a math instructor with a reputation as being a great teacher.

Deacon Rodgers, The People's Community Baptist Church in Silver Spring, Maryland, under the pastoral ministry of Reverend Dr. Haywood Robinson, III, appreciates all that you do as a servant for mankind.

A Stalwart Man of God

Minister Ayize Sabater

A   Reverend Dr. Ayize Sabater, God has called you to minister and serve mankind under the leadership of the Holy Spirit.

Y   You have demonstrated that your life's purpose rests on believing God's Word and doing it in your life.

I   In your heart is a melody of praise to God for your

Z   zealous use of social entrepreneurism, which is highly compatible with the values, beliefs, and goals of an experienced chief executive officer with a demonstrated history of working in the primary/ secondary industry. As an

E   experienced chief executive officer, your

S   service to mankind consists of helping start the Montessori School of Early Childhood Education

Program. You also serve as a board member of Montessori for Social Justice with a mission to support the creation of sustainable learning environments that dismantle systems of oppression and cultivate partnerships to liberate human potential. As a research assistant at Morgan State University, Baltimore, Maryland, God has blessed you also in this service to mankind.

A   According to Luke 6:38 (NIV), "Give, and it will be given to you. A good measure, pressed down, shaken together and running over, will be poured into your lap. For with the measure you use, it will be measured to you." 2 Chronicles 15:7 states,

B   "But as for you, be strong and do not give up, for your work will be rewarded." You have served in high esteem

A   as an Associate Minister at The People's Community Baptist Church, Silver Spring, Maryland under the anointed leadership of Reverend Dr. Haywood Robinson, III. Presently, God has given you the position of head of Willow Oak Montessori School in North Carolina. Your background shows

T   that you received a Bachelor of Arts degree from Morehouse College, 1992, Master of Divinity degree from Wesley Theological Seminary, 1999, and Doctor of Education in Urban Education and Leadership from Morgan State University, 2018. As a stalwart servant, your soul is

E   eager for the

R   race.

Minister Ayize Sabater, you are a stalwart man of God who is blessed with a wonderful family. You and your wife, Rhonda, have five children who can model positive traits from their parents. They have memories of their father's innovative social justice work that positioned him to be featured as the keynote speaker for American University's freshman class in 2009 and a 2010 recipient of a White House award for your non-profit organization, which was presented by First Lady, Michelle Obama. In 2014 you authored a book, *Tellin' Children Our Story: A Fun Technique for Teaching History...* God has blessed you to lecture internationally on cultural empowerment.

Thank God for your faithfulness. You are truly a stalwart man of God as you reach out to others for a better life.

(Ayize [I-E-zay] Sabater)

A Stalwart Pastor of God

Pastor Dotty Schmitt

P   Pastor Dotty Schmitt, praises to God is always in your heart.

A   A transition from misery to joy is your lot.

S   Sound theology from the book of Philippians is your passion given by God each day.

T   To keep on teaching and doing it God's way.

O   Oh, how wonderful to know that life's challenges and sorrows

R   rest with God for a greater tomorrow.

S   Sound teaching of the goodness of God you give so we can receive, if we trust and obey.

C   Challenges you present to do it God's way.

H   Heavy hearts can be reduced if we believe God and follow through by

M   meditating on the joy, God's way.

I   In your heart is an anointed touch from God each day.

T   To teach and pray and

T   to do it God's way.

Pastor Dotty Schmitt, you are a noble woman of God who cultivates the hunger for God's Word when you teach. You also create within your students a desire to study God's Word. You teach God's Word by magnifying God so that we see Him more fully and celebrate His incomparable worthiness and grace.

As a teacher of God's Word, you connect God's Word with life so that we will conform to the likeness of Christ with ever-increasing glory by the Holy Spirit.

I have witnessed two Bible study classes under your tutelage and I thank you for cultivating the hunger of God's Word within me.

1 Peter 2:2 tells us to, "...desire the sincere milk of the word..."

Pastor Dotty Schmitt, one of your books, *Stand on My Shoulder* is a "...nail in a sure place..." (Isa. 22:23) for families, churches, and communities. Your emphasis on the next generation brings joy to one's heart and soul because of its focus on the Word of God. God has given you the gift to plant roots in one's heart with biblical truth. Your spiritual wisdom comes through knowing the gospel. You and your husband, Reverend Dr. Charles Schmitt, are international teachers, going to Israel annually as well as to other nations. In 1983, the two of you founded Immanuel's Church in Silver Spring, Maryland. This church is multicultural with people from sixty-five different nations.

Both of you have a passion to see an outpouring of the Holy Spirit on the earth and to witness the promised worldwide harvest of souls that will pave the return of our Lord Jesus.

God has blessed you and your husband with three daughters, devoted sons-in-law, and five grandchildren.

Thank you for your service to mankind.

A Stalwart Woman of God

Lottie Scott

L   Lottie Scott, you are a remarkable mother to your son who has a disability. He is now an adult and you give him the best care as his caregiver.

O   Only God gives you the strength year after year to give him the best of care. Matthew 6:34 (NIV) tells us,

T   "Therefore do not worry about tomorrow, for tomorrow will worry about itself. Each day has enough trouble of its own."
Psalms 35:6 (NIV)

T   tells us, "May their path be dark and slippery, with the angel of the Lord pursuing them." Your

I   insight kept your eyes casted upon Jesus on your journey.

E   Even when things looked stressful, God gave you

S   strength to carry on because you

C cast all your cares on Him. Psalms 25:6 (NIV) guided you to "Remember,

O O Lord, thy tender mercies and thy loving kindnesses..." It gave you the faith to

T take care of your son's physical needs, including preparing meals and other logical tasks such as driving him to the doctor and keeping the house clean. Your son knows that he is loved and accepted. Psalms 26:2-3 (NIV)

T "Test me, Lord, and try me, examine my heart and my mind; for I have always been mindful of your unfailing love and have lived in reliance on your faithfulness."

Lottie Scott, you are a stalwart woman of God who understands what your son is going through. You are attentive, dependable, and trustworthy. Thank God for your faithfulness. When your son was thirty-four years old, he was diagnosed with Neurosarcoidosis, a chronic disease of the central nervous system.

Your records show that you graduated from Norfolk State University with a major in early childhood education. You also did graduate work toward your master's degree. You taught thirty-three years at Camelot Elementary School in Chesapeake, Virginia.

May God continue to lead and guide you as a devoted mother and lifelong caregiver for your son.

A Stalwart Woman of God

Deaconess Carolyn Shackleford

C   Carolyn Shackleford, you live life to the fullest because

A   along life's journey you find

R   restoration serving as a deaconess, caregiver member, and member of the Human Resources Ministry.

O   Only God provides you the energy to

L   live life as an exciting, challenging adventure.

Y   You are important; there is

N   nobody like you! Because you

S   smile often to see the

H   humor in all kinds of situations. You

A   allow yourself to be happy because life happens in the form of

C   changes and we can't stop them. Carolyn,

K   keep on standing up for yourself, continue to

L   live a life of serving to benefit others because life is an
E   exciting, challenging adventure to live by faith to its
F   fullest.
O   Only God and His Son, Jesus Christ, will give you a
    better tomorrow.
R   Remember,
D   don't give up but remember all the benefits and services
    you have done for others.

Deaconess Carolyn Shackleford, you are a stalwart woman of God. You show God's love when you reach out to others. You rely on Isaiah 41:10 (NIV), "So do not fear, for I am with you, do not be dismayed, for I am your God. I will strengthen you and help you. I will uphold you with my righteous right hand."

Thank you Deaconess Shackleford for exhibiting your radiant faith through Christ.

A Stalwart Man of God

Dr. Allan Smith

Retired Superintendent of the Edenton, North Carolina School District

A   Dr. Allan Smith, I shall always remember you as an outstanding superintendent of the Edenton, North Carolina School District when my husband was pastor at Warren Grove Missionary Baptist Church from 1978 through 2011. Your

L   leadership approved programs that our church provided for students in grades three, four, and five throughout the Edenton-Chowan Schools. The main focus was to provide direct instruction to those students who scored the lowest on the reading and math sections of the North Carolina State standards tests. This initiative resulted in improved test scores and the best scores ever made by the students in Edenton-Chowan Schools. Your

L   leadership also consisted of being present and speaking at our parent seminars and workshops, Christian Education Programs, and Black Male Programs. You will

A   always be remembered as a great communicator who moved your district's vision forward. You maintained

N   noteworthy, top-notch educational programs for your students. Your

S   strategic communications advice involved others in the decision-making process.

M   My husband and I were involved in this process. Your

I   interpersonal skills brought out the best in people. Your

T   tailored programs infinitely improved students' academic, vocational, social, and mental development.

H   High expectations and standards were maintained.

Dr. Allan Smith, you are a stalwart man of God.

Thank God for all that you did when you were superintendent of the Edenton Public Schools in Edenton, North Carolina. You always put God first. Matthews 6:33 says that above all things in our lives, we should seek God, and everything else will be provided for us. As important as education is, it should never come before our relationship with God. You put God in front of all your concerns. That's why you are a stalwart man of God.

Your records show that in 1992, you received the Doctor of Education (EdD) in Educational Leadership at Auburn University, Auburn, Alabama. In 1987, you received the Post-Graduate Certificate in Educational Supervision and Administration from Troy State University in Troy, Alabama. In 1976, you earned a Master of Science in Specific Learning Disabilities and Certification in School Psychometry from Troy State University, Troy, Alabama. In 1973, you completed a Bachelor of Science in Mental Retardation from Troy State University, Troy, Alabama.

Dr. Smith is married to his lovely wife, Nancy Hutto Smith. They have two children, Gretchen and Mark. Their daughter, Gretchen Anne Smith, is married to Jeff Kirby. Their son, Mark Joseph Smith, is married to Cynthia Young Smith.

God has blessed Dr. Smith and Nancy with four grandchildren: Brandon Errico, Emily Errico, Lauren Smith, and Parker Smith.

Thank God for you, Dr. Smith, and your service to mankind. You and Nancy will always have a special place in my heart.

A Stalwart Woman of God

Annie Smith

A   Annie Smith, I shall always remember you as one of my best teachers at Suburban Park Elementary School in Norfolk, Virginia. You put your whole self into carrying out assignments bestowed upon you. As my Black History Coordinator, you showcased black history in February and other teachers were motivated to do the same. Because of your wisdom, our students participated in the city-wide Black History Contest and our school won first place.

N   Nothing stops you or puts you down. I reflect to 2000 through 2004 when you and your husband, Howard, your sister, Linda, and two of my other teachers, Myra Wallace and Rilene Brookins, traveled from Chesapeake, Virginia, and Virginia Beach to my husband's church in Edenton, North Carolina to participate in our acceleration program held on Saturdays. The main focus was to provide direct instruction to those students who scored the lowest on the reading and math sections of the North Carolina State standards tests. This initiative resulted in improved test scores, and according to the superintendent, the best scores ever. Annie, you have shared with me that you prayed

N   new mercies each and every day for your students. I believe Psalms 32:8 (NIV) was in your spirit concerning your students,

I   "I will instruct you and...counsel you with my loving eye on you."

E   Even after you retired as a teacher, you continued to embody qualities of excellence.

S   Something within you
M   makes you stand tall.
I   In the presence of God
T   there is no room to fall.
H   Heaven shines on you, so keep doing it God's way and stand tall.

Annie Smith, you are a strong, stalwart woman of God. You have made many achievements as a teacher and author to mankind.

Your book *Been Through the Storms* gives the reader ways to cope with life. As a retired teacher, God has not finished with you yet because presently, you are orchestrating a play for seniors, ages seventy, eighty, and ninety years old.

You graduated from Norfolk State College in 1965, now Norfolk State University, with a B.S. degree in Education. Further studies were obtained from the University of Virginia and Old Dominion University in Norfolk, Virginia.

Annie, you and Howard are blessed with two children, Karl and Wayne Smith. Karl and his wife, Katherine, have given you three grandchildren, Kole, age four, Kinsey, age six, and Kara, age two. Wayne and his wife, Takiesha, have two children, Jonathan, age seventeen, and Victoria, age nineteen.

Your children and grandchildren live in Fishers, Indiana.

Karl has a career as a material requirements planning controller for Rolls Royce. Wayne is a Cloud Solution Architect for Microsoft.

Thank God for your family and your service to mankind.

A Stalwart Woman of God

Kathryn Torrence

K   Kathryn Torrence, the records show that you have been affiliated with the David M. Simpson Law Firm for thirty years in the Greenbelt, Maryland area. With a background in criminal law, you have a great deal of experience

A   about how to relate to clients and their problems. Being under the

T   teaching of a super lawyer, you relate to clients about their problems and show respect to them about what they are facing. Being a child of God, you

H   have prayed with clients and mentored their families. When you

R   relate to the *least of these*, you are serving as God's disciple. God leads

Y you to talk to clients and pray with them. Remember that 1 John 1:9 says, "If we confess of our sins, he is faithful and just to forgive us our sins, and to cleanse us from all unrighteousness." John 12:6 (NASB) says,

N "Now he said this, not because he was concerned about the poor, but because he was a thief, and as he had the money box, he used to pilfer what was put into it."

T The Holy Spirit leads you to mentor to clients.

O Only God leads you to handle cases so your clients can get on with their lives and leave troubles in the past. Because you work for God, you get good

R results and your clients would leave feeling better. God also gave you good

R results when you got to know your clients who put their trust in your hand. Because God directed you to work with clients, they

E experienced

N new directions God's way and a

C compassion to

E eliminate crime.

Kathryn Torrence, you are a stalwart woman of God. When God directed your path and life journey, God gave you guidance and your faith. As a Christian, the Bible was your book of faith and practice. God prepared you for the mission.

In 1981, you graduated from George Mason University with a Bachelor of Arts degree.

You are an active member of The People's Community Baptist Church in Silver Spring, Maryland under the anointed pastoral ministry of Reverend Dr. Haywood Robinson, III. You are the co-chair of the Scholarship and Christian Education Ministry.

God bless you for your faithfulness.

Postscript

God has blessed you with two children, Kamry Morissa Smith and Jeremiah Baltimore. Kamry is married to Roy Smith and they have a beautiful daughter, Kendall Rose Smith. Jeremiah graduated from Temple University, May 17, 2020. He will attend law school in the fall of 2020 to major in criminal justice.

A Stalwart Woman of God

Brenda Ward

B   Brenda Ward, you are a stalwart woman of God who was born in England. However, to date, you have spent most of your life in Canada, and now, secondly, in the United States of America. In the

R   radiance of God's love, you have always reached out to others because your life

E   entails encouraging others to soar above life's trials.

N   Nobody but God has given you the gift of daily inspirational writing and serving others. The

D   divine miracle worker is still working in you. 1 Peter 4:10-11 (ESV) states,

A   "As each has received a gift, use it to serve one another, as good stewards of God's varied grace: whoever speaks, as one who speaks oracles of God; whoever serves, as one who serves by the strength that God supplies--in order that in everything God may be glorified through Jesus Christ. To him belong glory and dominion forever and ever. Amen."

God made it possible for you to

W   work as a senior administrative assistant with the International Monetary Fund (IMF). The IMF is an international organization headquartered in Washington, D.C., consisting of 189 countries working to foster global monetary cooperation, and secure financial stability.

A   Along your life journey, you are a prayer warrior, teacher of creative stitchery, executive secretary to Reverend Dr. Haywood Robinson, III, pastor of The People's Community Baptist Church. You also assist in the Christian Education Program, and are a member of the Music Ministry.

R   Reaching out to others is your theme song. This is expressed as an outgrowth of your leading the Prayer Stitch Ministry when you give your gifts to residents of nursing homes, hospital patients, and babies in hospitals.

D   Down in your heart is a melody that expresses for God to use your earthly vessel. Psalms 100:3 (NIV) states, "Know that the Lord is God. It is he that made us, and we are his; we are his people, and the sheep of his pasture."

Sister Brenda Ward, you are a stalwart woman of God wherever you go. Even though you were born in England and are a citizen of the United States, you also have citizenship in Canada, and in St. Kitts and Nevis. You let your light shine in the hearts of people. Hebrews 6:10 (NIV) tells us, "God is not unjust; he will not forget your work and the love you have shown him as you have helped his people and continue to help them."

Thank God for your service to mankind.

Postscript

You have two children. Your son, his wife, and their three sons live in Canada. Your daughter has two sons.

You received a Bachelor of Science degree in Business Administration from the University of the West Indies.

A Stalwart Woman of God

Deaconess Tawana Lewis Wheeler

T   Deaconess Tawana Lewis Wheeler, God has given you the desire to consecrate your life to a life of service. 1 Peter 4:10-11 (ESV) tells us,

A   "As each has received a gift, use it to serve one another, as good stewards of God's varied grace..." Ephesians 2:10 (ESV) tells us, "For we are his

W   workmanship, created in Christ Jesus for good works, which God prepared beforehand, that we should walk in them." You are involved in

A   an array of services and ministries. Your leadership and service at The People's Community Baptist Church, Silver Spring, Maryland under the pastoral ministry of Reverend Dr. Haywood Robinson, III, consists of services as deaconess, Tuesday night Bible study teacher, VerticaL PraiZe team member, Chancel Choir member, prayer intercessor/moderator and mission short-term volunteer. In the

N   name of Jesus, you are strong, sturdy, dependable, and courageous.

A   Along your life service to mankind, nothing stops you. You are

L   loyal to the Church and

E   eager to serve wherever you are needed. 1 Corinthians 1:30 (NIV) says, "It is because of him that you are in Christ Jesus, who has become for us wisdom from God- that is, our righteousness, holiness and redemption." You serve from your heart

W   with the love of God, you are equipped for the work of ministry. 1 Peter 4:10 (ESV) tells us, "As each has received a gift, use it to serve one another, as good stewards of God's varied grace...." You use your spiritual gifts according to Romans 12:6-8 (ESV),

I   "...in proportion to our faith; if service, in our serving; the one who teaches, in his teaching; the one who exhorts, in his exhortation; the one who contributes, in generosity; the one who leads, with zeal; the one who does acts of mercy, with cheerfulness." According to 1 Peter 4:9-10 (ESV) you,

S   "Show hospitality to one another without grumbling. As each has received a gift, use it to serve one another, as good stewards of God's varied grace..." Tawana Lewis Wheeler, you are a light of the

W world. You let your light shine before others, so that they may see your good work. The

H Holy Spirit is your teacher. You pursue

E excellence in loving others and laboring for God because the grace you display through Jesus Christ keeps you moving forward. Your plans are

E established because you commit your work to the Lord. Your

L love for God and His Son, Jesus Christ,

E encourages you to pursue excellence. You have the will to live and

R run the race for God.

Deaconess Tawana Lewis Wheeler, you are a stalwart woman of God. You follow the one who is the author and the finisher of our faith.

Your records show that you had a career as a healthcare administrator throughout Washington, D.C. and Maryland. You have received two undergraduate degrees, A.A.S. in Respiratory Therapy, and a B.S. in Vocational Education. This background supported you as a clinician and instructor in respiratory care for over thirty years.

Records also show that you received a Master of Public Administration (MPA) in Healthcare from Troy University as a career change.

Your experience in healthcare has afforded the opportunities to work especially with women and children to meet their health needs domestically and globally.

Records also show that you are the mother of one daughter and the grandmother of two grandchildren.

God bless you for your service to mankind.

Remembering Stalwart Men and Women of the Past

By Audrey W. Mills
(Written January 1975)
Dr. H.W. B. Walker, Pastor
Deacon Wilbert Mills, Chairman
**Honorary Service for Members 50 Years
or More in Service**
"UNFORGETTABLE MOMENTS"
"Doing It Their Way"

God granted us the following:
Sheep to brighten and strengthen our flock.
Their gifts and talents alike;
Have left an everlasting spark.

Leola, Mary, Lubertia, Ruth, Lillie G.,
James R., Maggie, Virginia, Georgia, and Rella
Are special persons in their own rights.
God has truly blessed each one
Through these many days and nights.

The history of Second Calvary
Is found within each, as our records unfold.
The halls of these pages;
Give you a glimpse of precious lives to be told.

Today and each day;
As they tarry along;
Strong, serene, we must say
Thank you, God, for each honoree.
For letting them do it their way.

LEOLA CLARK is at her best,

When she is MCing a program at your request.
At a moment's notice, she is at your call,
Ready to speak above them all.
Yes, Leola, you are our
Mistress of Ceremony Queen, any old day.
You have 50 years more to do it your way.

MARY DAVENPORT, alias, "Maggie" so fine and true

Will come to your rescue regardless of your hue.
Ann Landers is second best to Maggie's advice.
She will set you straight concerning Women's Day
For all of us know she'll do it her way.
So alias, Maggie, so fine and true,
Second Calvary appreciates what you do.
The records show that you stand behind what you do and say.
Keep on trucking, Maggie, and do it your way.

LUBERTIA GREEN, Florence Nightingale was she.

Idella, Mary Frances, and all the other little
Spruiells she would take upon her knee.
Her soft touch but firm demands,
We will never forget as we stroll down memory lane.
You may think that she has little to say;
Cornelius Green, she loves so dearly.
"Yes Darling, Honey, and Sweetie Pie,
You have no need to fret or cry.
I am here with you each and every day."
Now we understand how Lubertia does it her way.

JAMES R. JONES - if given an inch

Will take a mile for the black man's defense.
Mr. NAACP--A Man of Civil Rights

Helped to fight our battle with all his might.
You have lived a life with fortitude and pride.
Love for your people that was justified.
God bless you, "Jimmy".
We salute you today.
Keep on fighting and do it your way.

RUTH LAND, fashionable as you can see,

Could win a place on the cover of *Ebony*.
She is always well dressed and well-groomed.
For one day shocking and alarming,
We're going to get the news about
Ruth's Prince Charming.
No one will know what to say, for
Ruth would have done it her way.
This is not an announcement about
Ruth, the trustee.
We are only joking you see.
When Ruth breaks the news on D-Day,
Reverend will announce, "Praise the Lord.
She did it her way."

MAGGIE OSBORNE of the Deaconess Board

Is as sharp as a two-edged sword.
She keeps up with the latest styles

Always glamorous with that lovely smile.
Her record shows an age of three scores plus nineteen.
Quite a record for a Beauty Queen.
So hats off to you, Maggie, "Ole!"
Keep on doing it your way.

RELLA MAYFIELD, our Mother of the Church.

You will never find another like her
Wherever you search.
She's a guiding light and a living star
Who stretches out her love so very far.
Mother Mayfield, forgive us, if you may,
For joking with you for what I am about to say.
You really don't act your age the way
You strut with your cane.
So let me take you down memory lane.
Remember when you said, "Let the young man take
your arm."
Were you serious or were you using your charm?
You are always together from head to toe.
Your motto is never, "anything goes."
We realize that you are beautiful in every way.
You are a special kind of person and you do it your way,
By setting examples for the young and old,
Something one can't buy with silver or gold.
Seriously speaking, we love you each and every day.

Keep using your walking cane and do it your way.

LILLIE G. WINFIELD, a genius in disguise

Is so naïve that she can't recognize
That she is a jack of all trades.
From her head to her feet,
Whatever she does it's hard to beat.
Her famous last words
Are, "Well folks, I stand before you again
Asking for your support, so don't let me down.
For you never do.
Can we depend on you?"
These famous words are usually followed
With a big grin.
For this is the secret to each win.
Lillie G. Winfield, without dismay, can win you
Over because she does it her way.

VIRGINIA RANDOLPH, Sojourner Truth,

Loves her church and pastor, too.
Her history reveals such a beautiful story
With success, failure, and achievements
Without vain glory.
Right now what is so dear to her heart
Is Virginia Seminary and she urges us to start

To do our part and support a great program today.
Her announcements and speeches show
She's doing it her way.
Virginia works hard with the Helping Hands and
Missionaries, too.
This is why we named her Sojourner Truth.
She is one person whom we can say
Is thoughtful and helpful each and every day.
For this is how Virginia Randolph
Does it her way.

GEORGIA RUFFIN, the Usher Board Queen,

Rears each usher as he or she comes on the scene.
Keeping you in line with an iron hand.
When she finishes with you,
One knows where he or she stands.
She served us well and we love her so.
Her standards we will carry wherever we go.
Continue your reign, Georgia, from your pew.
For it helps to carry us through.
We are ready to listen to whatever
You say.
For we know you are doing it
Your way.

Conclusions

*L*ife is difficult but when we deal with life's difficulties, we build invaluable strength. This strength enables us to successfully fulfill our deepest, most meaningful purposes. When times are tough, we must be tougher. Pray to God for the strength to endure a tough life that leads to greatness.

When you tune in to God, you quiet yourself down and you fix your spiritual eyes on Jesus.

Even when we do all the right things in life, don't make the mistake of forgetting God. Don't live as if the world is your all and all. For example, working as a successful employee, in good health, with a good social life, sleeping eight hours every night, never smoking or drinking, and sticking to routines to stay healthy, such as walking, exercising, etc. Despite all this, don't live as if the world *is* all.

Jeremiah 8:20 (ESV) reminds us, "The harvest is past, the summer is ended, and we are not saved." You may live a full life filled with meaning and prayer, and pursuit and fulfillment, and satisfaction, yet you forget God.

James 4:14 answers the question, "What is the meaning of life?" James gives this answer, "...It is even a vapour, that appeareth for a little time, and then vanisheth away." Some folks live only for material possessions, things you can touch and feel, pleasure, but are not living for the spiritual.

A great way to change your thoughts is to appreciate and enjoy what you already have. Enjoy whatever amount of success you have achieved instead of feeling sad about what you have not been able to achieve. There is nothing wrong with always fixing higher benchmarks or goals, but failure to reach them should not spoil your enjoyment of what you already have.

The time to be happy is today because yesterday has already passed and you cannot be sure that tomorrow will bring any happiness.

Don't depend on material possessions to create happiness for you. It is for you to choose to be happy, whatever the situation.

Wake up each day with God on your mind. Resolve to stay happy during the day. Pray to God to keep you in perfect peace and resolve to remain calm as soon as you sense trouble coming. You owe yourself an ethical duty to remain happy.

Endnotes

1 Mark and Patti Virkler, Communion With God Ministries, "A 7 Step Meditation Process Explored", https://www.cwg-ministries.org/7-step-meditation-process-explored (last accessed January 31, 2020).

2 Rhonda Jones, "What Is Spiritual Lifelessness," The Christian Mediator, Spiritual Lifelessness | Get More In Touch with Your Spiritual Side, https://thechristianmeditator.com/what-is-spiritual-lifelessness/ (last accessed January 25, 2020).

3 Allen Parr, "5 Ways to Handle Spiritual Dryness", https://www.allenparr.com/5-ways-to-handle-spiritual-dryness/ (last accessed January 31, 2020).

4 Ibid.

5 Ibid.

6 Ibid.

7 John N. Clayton, "What is the Fabric of Life?," Does God Exist? Bi-Monthly Journal, Volume 24, Number 4, July/August 1997, https://www.doesgodexist.org/JulAug97/

WhatIsTheFabricOfLife.html (last accessed January 25, 2020).

8   Ibid.

9   Ibid.

10 Ibid.

11 American Heritage Dictionary, Second College ed., s.v. "tapestry."

12 Matt Reacher, Color Psychology Meaning, The Psychology of Colors, "Colors of the Rainbow & their Meanings," November 3, 2015, https://colorpsychologymeaning.com/the-colors-of-the-rainbow/ (last accessed April 21, 2020).